I0012592

Technologies

WebGPU
Gone Wrong
Why Software Projects Fails

**Analysing the conflict and challenges
around the WebGPU API**

Kenwright

BOOK TITLE:
WebGPU Gone Wrong
(First Edition)
ISBN-13: 979-8-34-020381-6

Edition: 12019121240

Preface

Is WebGPU a dream? Or is it a car crash? When WebGPU was first announced, it promised to revolutionize graphics on the web. Developers and tech enthusiasts alike were eager for a future where GPU-accelerated web applications would be faster, more efficient, and more powerful than ever before. But reality hasn't quite lived up to the hype.

Beneath the sleek surface, WebGPU is riddled with issues that can't be ignored. Security vulnerabilities leave it exposed in ways that could put users at risk. The shader language - meant to be the heart of this new technology - is supported almost nowhere else, creating a steep barrier to entry for developers. Worse yet, WebGPU struggles with robustness and compatibility, meaning what works in one environment may fall apart in another.

In writing WebGPU Gone Wrong, my goal is not to dismiss the potential of WebGPU, but to bring to light the flaws that have been glossed over. This book is a casual dive into the dark side of WebGPU - examining its critical failings in security, robustness, cross-platform support, and overall usability.

This isn't a story of outright failure. It's a story of broken promises and missed opportunities, but also of hope - because understanding these problems is the first step toward fixing them. For developers, tech leaders, and anyone invested in the future of web technologies, this book offers a frank and necessary exploration of WebGPU's flaws and the steps needed to make it the tool it could be.

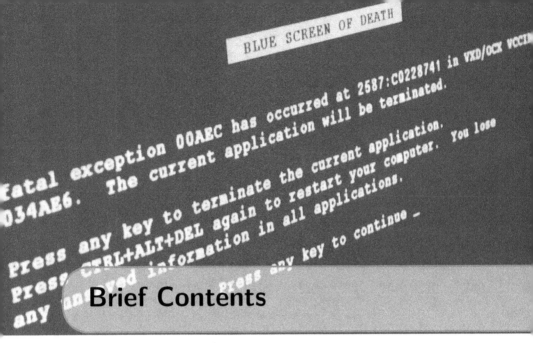

BLUE SCREEN OF DEATH

Fatal exception 00AEC has occurred at 2587:C0228741 in VXD/OCX VCCI 034AE6. The current application will be terminated.

Press any key to terminate the current application. Press CTRL+ALT+DEL again to restart your computer. You lose any unsaved information in all applications.

Press any key to continue –

Brief Contents

Content

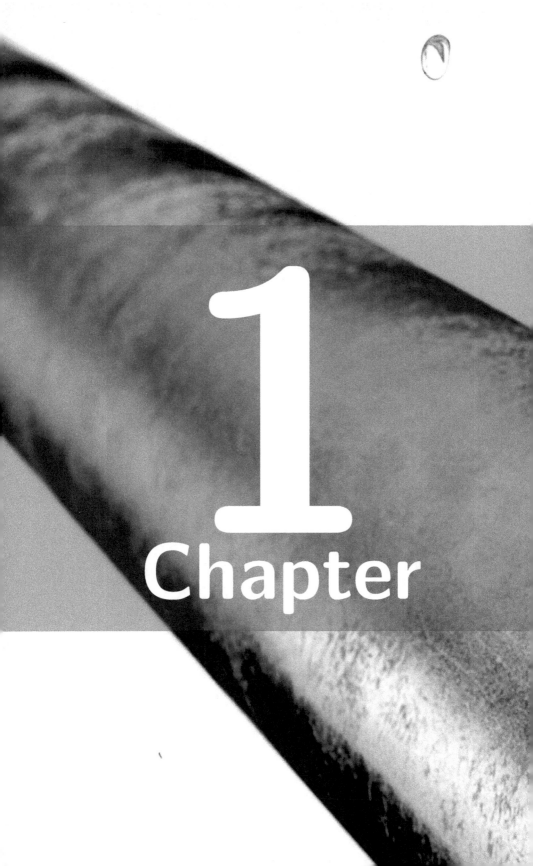

1
Chapter

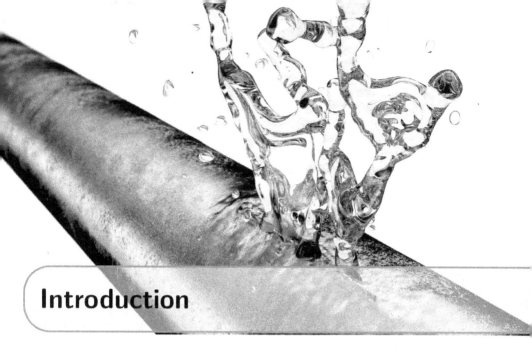

Introduction

Quote: "I have not failed. I've just found 10,000 ways that won't work."
(**Thomas Edison**)

1.1 Introduction

NEW is always scary! It's human nature to avoid change - we get used to what we know! And what we know is WebGL! It's been around forever - and it does its job. So why go and upset things with a new API called WebGPU? Did the web need a new API or was their sinister reasons driving the push for a new standard?

Is WebGPU the 'Titanic' of the web? (designed to be unsinkable)

Without a doubt, the rise of WebGPU marks a pivotal moment in the evolution of web technologies. As a powerful new API designed to bring low-level GPU access to the web, WebGPU promises to revolutionize how developers create complex graphical applications and high-performance computing tasks directly in the browser. However, with these promises come a host of challenges, misconceptions, and overlooked risks. This book explores the deeper implications of WebGPU, shedding light on the complexities, pitfalls, and realities that have been glossed over in the excitement surrounding its introduction.

For developers, WebGPU presents both an opportunity and a dilemma. While it unlocks unprecedented control over hardware, it also introduces steep learning curves, fragmented support, and security risks that are far from trivial. This book dives into these technical intricacies, examining the practical hurdles developers face when adopting WebGPU, from performance issues to debugging nightmares. Alongside technical analysis, this book offers a critical lens on the motivations behind WebGPU's creation, questioning who truly benefits from this shift in web development and what the long-term consequences might be.

We also explore the often-overlooked economic and market forces driving WebGPU's adoption. While it is presented as an open standard, its development is shaped by powerful corporations with significant financial interests in hardware sales and cloud services. This book uncovers the ways in which WebGPU may push developers and consumers alike into expensive hardware upgrades, thereby fueling a never-ending cycle of technological obsolescence.

Food for Thought - Innovative Technologies That Fell Short: **Nintendo Virtual Boy** (1995) - A 3D Gaming Console That Gave Players a Headache - Nintendo's Virtual Boy promised an immersive 3D experience, but its poor execution, uncomfortable design, and lack of games made it a commercial disaster.

This book is not only for those working directly with WebGPU, but also for anyone interested in the broader impact of technological shifts in the web development landscape. By analyzing WebGPU through technical, economic, and social lenses, we aim to provide a comprehensive view of its potential—and its pitfalls. As with any new technology, WebGPU promises much, but understanding its limitations is key to making informed decisions about its use.

1.2 Summary

The chapters ahead are designed to give readers a balanced and detailed understanding of what WebGPU is, how it works, and why its introduction is more complicated than it seems. Each chapter dissects a different facet of WebGPU, from performance issues to security concerns, offering insights grounded in real-world examples and practical experience. Whether you're a seasoned developer, a technology enthusiast, or a curious observer of the tech industry's latest trends, this book will guide you through the complexities of WebGPU and help you navigate its rapidly evolving landscape.

2

Chapter

The WebGPU Mirage: Hype vs. Reality

Quote: "The real problem is not whether machines think but whether men do." (**B.F. Skinner**)

2.1 Introduction

WebGPU was introduced with much fanfare, promising to usher in a new era of graphics rendering on the web. Positioned as the successor to WebGL, WebGPU was touted as a revolutionary API that would offer developers more direct access to the GPU, reduce bottlenecks, and deliver unmatched performance. Its potential to bring desktop-level graphics to web applications excited developers, gamers, and content creators alike. At its inception, WebGPU was heralded as the key to unlocking more advanced 3D graphics, immersive virtual experiences, and higher-performance web applications.

2.1.1 Marketing vs. Reality: Where the Excitement Came From

The excitement surrounding WebGPU didn't just stem from its technical potential; it was heavily fueled by an aggressive marketing campaign. Tech companies and major players in the hardware industry championed WebGPU as the technology of the future, promising to solve the limitations of existing APIs. Marketing materials painted a picture of effortless integration, massive performance gains, and smooth compatibility across devices. These promises resonated with developers and users alike, creating an anticipation that went beyond what the technology was truly ready to deliver.

2.1.2 Unrealistic Expectations: How the Hype Grew Out of Control

As more developers bought into the vision of WebGPU, expectations began to spiral. The hype, driven by speculative articles, overzealous presentations, and promises of a "next-gen" web experience, created a wave of unrealistic assumptions. Many expected WebGPU to not only replace WebGL but to outperform it in every possible way, all while being simple to implement. These inflated expectations overlooked the fact that WebGPU was still in its infancy, and much of its potential remained theoretical rather than practical. The gap between what WebGPU promised and what it could realistically deliver began to widen, setting the stage for disappointment.

Food for Thought - Innovative Technologies That Fell Short: **Microsoft Zune** (2006) - The iPod Killer That Couldn't Compete - Entering the market too late, the Zune failed to offer enough differentiation from Apple's iPod and never managed to capture the attention of music lovers.

2.2 Performance: Fact or Fiction?

2.2.1 Promised Speed Gains: What Was Supposed to Happen

From the outset, WebGPU was positioned as a major leap forward in performance. Advocates promised speed gains due to its ability to give developers more direct control over the GPU, minimizing the overhead seen in WebGL and other higher-level APIs. WebGPU was supposed to eliminate many of the inefficiencies found in WebGL's abstractions, offering a streamlined path for processing complex shaders and computations. Developers were led to believe that WebGPU would provide the kind of low-level GPU access typically seen in native applications, making the web a truly competitive platform for high-performance graphics.

2.2.2 The Reality of Performance: Why the Results Fall Short

Despite the bold promises, real-world performance gains from WebGPU have been less dramatic than expected. While the API does provide more control over the GPU, this increased control comes at the cost of greater complexity, leading to development overhead that can negate the supposed speed improvements. Additionally, WebGPU's current implementation across browsers is inconsistent, resulting in performance variability that developers find difficult to predict or optimize for. In many cases, developers who expected seamless boosts in rendering speed have encountered diminishing returns, with WebGPU offering little advantage over its predecessor, WebGL.

2.2.3 Misleading Benchmarks: How the Numbers Can Deceive

Performance benchmarks presented during WebGPU's early demonstrations painted an overly optimistic picture of its capabilities. These benchmarks often focused on specific, highly-optimized use cases that didn't represent the typical scenarios most developers would face. Furthermore, many of the touted speed gains were achieved under ideal conditions, without accounting for the complexity of real-world web applications. In practice, the performance improvements are often marginal, and in some cases, WebGPU performs worse due to the complexity of optimizing the API. This selective use of benchmarks has contributed to a skewed perception of what WebGPU can deliver.

2.3 The Compatibility Trap

2.3.1 Who's Really Left Behind: Hardware Compatibility Gaps

WebGPU's drive to push the boundaries of web graphics comes at a cost: reduced hardware compatibility. While WebGPU works well with the latest GPU technologies, it leaves many older devices behind. Devices that comfortably ran WebGL-based applications often struggle to meet the requirements of WebGPU, forcing users to upgrade their hardware or miss out on the benefits entirely. This selective compatibility undermines one of the core promises of the web: accessibility across a wide range of devices. By focusing on high-end GPUs, WebGPU effectively excludes a significant portion of users still operating older hardware.

2.3.2 Fragmentation Across Platforms: A Unified Standard That Isn't

While WebGPU was envisioned as a unified standard for web graphics, the reality is far more fragmented. Different browsers implement WebGPU in subtly different ways, leading to inconsistent performance and functionality across platforms. This lack of uniformity makes it difficult for developers to create truly cross-platform web applications, as what works seamlessly in one browser might break or perform poorly in another. The promise of a single, standardized API that runs everywhere remains elusive, with developers caught in the middle of a fragmented landscape that limits WebGPU's potential as a universal solution.

2.3.3 Legacy vs. Future: What Happens to Older Devices?

As WebGPU pushes forward, older devices and GPUs are being left in the dust. WebGL, with its broader hardware support, allowed developers to build applications that ran across a wide spectrum of devices, from high-end gaming rigs to low-end laptops and mobile phones. WebGPU, on the other hand, is built for the future, but this focus on cutting-edge technology means that legacy devices are increasingly incompatible. The result is a growing divide between users with the latest hardware and those with older systems, creating a fragmented web experience where some users are locked out of new features and applications.

2.4 Developer Experience: Hype vs. Hands-On

2.4.1 The Steep Learning Curve: Is WebGPU Really Easier?

One of the selling points of WebGPU was that it would be easier for developers to use, offering more intuitive control over GPU operations. In reality, however, WebGPU introduces a steep learning curve. Its low-level nature, while powerful, requires developers to manage far more complexity than they did with WebGL. Many developers, especially those used to higher-level abstractions, struggle to make sense of the intricate details of WebGPU. The API's complexity often leads to longer development times, more difficult debugging, and a steeper barrier to entry for new developers.

2.4.2 Abstraction Complexities: When Flexibility Becomes a Burden

While WebGPU offers developers more flexibility in how they interact with the GPU, this flexibility can quickly become a burden. The lack of high-level abstractions means that developers must manage many of the details that were previously handled by the API itself in WebGL. This added control can lead to more efficient code in theory, but in practice, it often results in longer development times and increased risk of introducing errors. The complexity of managing GPU resources, memory, and shaders can overwhelm developers, especially those working on smaller projects or without a deep understanding of low-level GPU operations.

2.4.3 Debugging Disasters: Why WebGPU Is Harder to Work With

One of the less-publicized downsides of WebGPU is the difficulty of debugging. While the API gives developers more control, it also removes many of the safety nets that existed in WebGL. Debugging GPU code is notoriously difficult, and WebGPU's low-level nature compounds this issue. Developers often find themselves spending hours trying to track down subtle bugs or performance issues, with limited tools available to assist them. The complexity of the API, combined with the lack of mature debugging tools, makes WebGPU a challenging environment to work in, even for experienced developers.

2.5 WebGPU's Delayed Impact

2.5.1 The Slow Road to Adoption: Why WebGPU Isn't Taking Over

Despite its promise, WebGPU has not seen the rapid adoption that many anticipated. Several factors contribute to this slow uptake, including the complexity of the API, inconsistent support across platforms, and the continued dominance of WebGL in existing applications. Many developers are hesitant to invest time and resources into learning WebGPU, given its current limitations and the significant changes it requires in their development workflows. As a result, WebGPU remains a niche technology, with its broader adoption delayed by the very challenges that were supposed to make it superior.

2.5.2 Unrealized Potential: Features That Still Aren't Working as Promised

WebGPU was supposed to introduce a host of features that would revolutionize web graphics, but many of these features are either still in development or don't work as smoothly as promised. Issues with browser implementations, incomplete support for certain GPU features, and ongoing development challenges have prevented WebGPU from reaching its full potential. Developers who were excited about using these cutting-edge features have often found themselves frustrated by missing functionality or incomplete documentation. This unrealized potential has led to a cautious approach from the development community, further slowing adoption.

2.5.3 Is WebGPU Ready for Prime Time? The Reality of Real-World Use

The question on many developers' minds is whether WebGPU is truly ready for widespread use. While it offers significant advancements in some areas, the challenges of performance variability, hardware compatibility, and developer complexity raise concerns about its readiness for prime time. Many real-world applications still rely heavily on WebGL, and the transition to WebGPU is far from seamless. Until these hurdles are addressed, WebGPU may remain more of a niche tool for advanced use cases rather than a mainstream solution for web graphics.

2.6 The Mirage Revealed

2.6.1 What the Hype Missed: Understanding WebGPU's True Role

In the rush to market WebGPU as a game-changer, many overlooked its true role within the broader ecosystem of web technologies. WebGPU is undeniably powerful, but its strengths lie in very specific use cases—primarily those that require direct, low-level access to the GPU. For most web developers, WebGPU may not replace WebGL or higher-level APIs anytime soon. Its complexity and hardware requirements make it a specialized tool rather than the universal solution it was often portrayed to be. Understanding this distinction is key to tempering expectations around its use.

2.6.2 Beyond the Smoke and Mirrors: Where WebGPU Can Actually Deliver

Despite its shortcomings, WebGPU does have real potential in certain areas. For developers working on cutting-edge applications, such as advanced 3D rendering, game development, or machine learning, WebGPU can deliver substantial performance improvements. Its ability to offer more granular control over the GPU allows for optimizations that simply aren't possible with WebGL. For those willing to navigate its complexities, WebGPU can unlock new levels of performance and flexibility in specific, high-performance use cases.

2.7 Summary

WebGPU was never going to be a perfect solution, and the hype surrounding it set unrealistic expectations. The reality is that no API can solve every problem, and WebGPU is no exception. While it offers powerful tools for certain tasks, it also comes with significant trade-offs. For most developers, the promise of WebGPU remains more of a mirage than a reality—at least for now. As the technology matures and its role becomes clearer, we may eventually see WebGPU fulfill some of its promises, but the perfect API remains as elusive as ever.

3
Chapter

Security Nightmares: WebGPU's Gaping Holes

Technology is a useful servant but a dangerous master. Christian Lous Lange

3.1 Introduction

WebGPU offers unprecedented power by giving web developers low-level access to the GPU, enabling advanced rendering and computational tasks directly from web browsers. However, this power comes with significant security risks. When an API provides deep system access, as WebGPU does, it inadvertently increases the potential for misuse. Hackers can exploit this access to run malicious code on GPUs, bypassing traditional CPU-focused security measures. The more control developers and applications have over hardware resources, the more opportunities exist for these controls to be exploited by bad actors.

3.1.1 Security by Design? Or a Forgotten Priority?

Security often takes a back seat in the rush to develop new technologies, and WebGPU is no exception. While WebGPU was designed with performance and flexibility in mind, it appears that security considerations were not as thoroughly integrated into the

API's design. WebGL, for all its limitations, benefitted from years of battle-tested security enhancements, such as secure context isolation and strict sandboxing. In contrast, WebGPU's rapid development may have led to security being deprioritized in favor of features, leaving critical vulnerabilities exposed.

3.1.2 How WebGPU Opens New Attack Vectors

WebGPU opens up entirely new avenues for potential attacks. By giving developers direct access to the GPU, it bypasses many of the traditional security protections that operate at the CPU level. For instance, WebGPU allows for low-level shader programming, which can be manipulated to perform tasks beyond graphics rendering, such as cryptojacking or data theft. Moreover, malicious scripts running within WebGPU could exploit GPU memory to access sensitive data or crash a system through denial of service (DoS) attacks. The exposure of this previously underutilized resource makes WebGPU a prime target for new categories of malware.

3.2 GPU Access: The New Attack Surface

3.2.1 Direct GPU Control: A Hacker's Dream

WebGPU offers developers the ability to interact with GPUs in a much more granular way than was possible with WebGL. While this level of control is great for performance, it also means that any vulnerabilities in the GPU or its drivers can be exploited by attackers. Malicious actors could craft shaders or workloads that overwhelm the GPU, or even worse, use this access to break out of the browser's security sandbox. Examples like the Spectre and Meltdown vulnerabilities have already shown how hardware-level access can be exploited. With WebGPU, hackers now have another potential route into users' systems.

3.2.2 Exploiting Low-Level Access: Risks in Shader Code

The ability to write low-level shader code in WebGPU is both a strength and a serious vulnerability. Shaders are programs that run on the GPU and can be exploited to perform unauthorized operations. For instance, a malicious shader could be crafted to execute hidden computations, effectively turning the GPU into a vehicle for cryptomining without the user's consent. Furthermore, malicious shaders could leak data or cause memory corruption, leading to crashes or, in some cases, allowing hackers to access privileged information stored in memory. The low-level nature of WebGPU means that such vulnerabilities are harder to detect and mitigate.

3.2.3 Memory Vulnerabilities: How WebGPU Can Be Compromised

Memory management has always been a critical security challenge, and WebGPU brings new complexities to this issue. With direct control over GPU memory, WebGPU applications could inadvertently—or maliciously—introduce memory vulnerabilities. For example, a poorly managed buffer could lead to out-of-bounds memory access, allowing attackers to manipulate or read data that should be protected. Furthermore, GPUs often share memory with CPUs, meaning that an exploit targeting GPU memory could potentially compromise the entire system. This kind of access expands the attack surface far beyond what was possible in previous generations of web technologies.

Food for Thought - Innovative Technologies That Fell Short: **Betamax** (1975) - Sony's Superior Technology, Defeated by VHS - Despite offering better quality, Betamax's short recording times and Sony's restrictive licensing allowed the inferior VHS format to dominate the home video market.

3.3 The Problem with Sandboxing

3.3.1 Inadequate Sandboxing: WebGPU's Weak Link

WebGPU's reliance on sandboxing is one of its biggest vulnerabilities. While browsers use sandboxing to isolate web applications from each other and from the underlying system, WebGPU's deep access to the GPU makes sandboxing less effective. Unlike WebGL, which was designed with stricter security boundaries, WebGPU opens a wider channel to the GPU, making it more difficult to enforce strict separation between processes. As a result, a compromised WebGPU application could potentially escape the sandbox, gaining access to system resources or other browser tabs.

3.3.2 Bypassing Browser Defenses: Why Current Protections Aren't Enough

Current browser defenses are largely designed around the assumptions made for higher-level APIs like WebGL, where direct hardware access is limited. WebGPU changes that equation by exposing more of the GPU's functionality to the browser, which makes existing security models inadequate. For example, standard cross-origin protections might not prevent a malicious WebGPU program from executing code that interacts with the system at a hardware level. While browser vendors have implemented basic safeguards, the rapid advancement of WebGPU means these defenses are constantly playing catch-up, leaving windows of vulnerability.

3.3.3 Case Studies: Sandboxing Failures in Similar Technologies

We've seen sandboxing failures in technologies similar to WebGPU, such as WebAssembly (Wasm) and WebGL. For example, WebAssembly has faced several challenges with escaping its sandbox environment due to improper handling of memory and unsafe code execution. WebGL has also experienced vulnerabilities where improper sandboxing allowed for denial of service (DoS) attacks or memory leaks. These cases highlight the risks inherent in any system where low-level hardware access is granted, making it clear that WebGPU's sandboxing must be especially robust to prevent similar failures.

3.4 Denial of Service and Resource Exhaustion

3.4.1 The Performance Trap: How Malicious Scripts Can Cripple Systems

One of WebGPU's key features—high-performance GPU access—can easily be turned against users. Malicious actors could write scripts designed to overload the GPU, effectively causing a denial of service (DoS) attack by consuming excessive resources. These scripts could run in the background of a seemingly harmless web page, crippling the user's system by monopolizing GPU time, overheating the hardware, or causing the browser to freeze. Because WebGPU allows such fine-grained control, these attacks could be more effective and harder to detect than traditional DoS attacks aimed at the CPU.

3.4.2 GPU Overload: Pushing Devices to the Breaking Point

WebGPU's design enables applications to push GPUs to their limits, but this can be a double-edged sword. Attackers could intentionally overload the GPU by submitting tasks that exceed the device's capacity, leading to thermal throttling, system crashes, or even hardware damage in extreme cases. This risk is particularly concerning for devices with weaker GPUs, such as laptops and mobile devices, which are more susceptible to performance degradation under heavy workloads. WebGPU's promise of high performance could thus be weaponized to create widespread disruption for users with less robust hardware.

3.4.3 Real-World DoS Scenarios: How WebGPU Could Enable Large-Scale Attacks

Denial of service attacks leveraging WebGPU could be scaled to affect large numbers of users simultaneously. For instance, a popular website could unknowingly host a WebGPU-based ad or widget containing malicious code that executes GPU-intensive operations. If this script is deployed across multiple browsers and devices, it could lead to widespread performance degradation or crashes, effectively creating a large-scale distributed denial of service (DDoS) attack. Examples from WebGL's past, where such attacks were possible through resource exhaustion, illustrate the potential danger WebGPU poses if left unregulated.

3.5 Cross-Platform Inconsistencies

3.5.1 The Danger of Fragmented Implementations: Security Gaps Between Browsers

One of the biggest challenges in WebGPU's development has been its inconsistent implementation across different browsers and platforms. Each browser handles WebGPU slightly differently, which leads to security gaps. A feature or bug in one browser's implementation might expose a vulnerability that doesn't exist in others, leading to a fragmented security landscape. These inconsistencies are especially dangerous because they provide hackers with multiple attack vectors—if one browser is secure, another might not be. This lack of uniformity weakens the overall security posture of WebGPU across the web.

3.5.2 Inconsistent Security Models: Why Different Platforms Lead to Vulnerabilities

Different platforms, such as Windows, macOS, and Linux, all implement WebGPU in their own ways, which can lead to vulnerabilities due to inconsistent security models. For example, a security feature that works on Windows may be poorly implemented or entirely absent on macOS, giving attackers a route to exploit the system. This inconsistency extends to hardware as well—GPUs from different manufacturers have different driver implementations, which means that WebGPU must account for varying levels of hardware security. This variance introduces additional risks that developers and security teams must consider when building cross-platform WebGPU applications.

3.5.3 Coordination Challenges: The Struggle to Maintain a Secure WebGPU Standard

Maintaining a secure and unified WebGPU standard across multiple platforms and browsers is a significant challenge. Coordinating between browser vendors, operating system developers, and GPU manufacturers requires constant communication and updates, but these stakeholders often operate on different timelines and priorities. This lack of coordination can lead to delays in security patches, leaving users vulnerable for extended periods. The complexity of keeping WebGPU secure across such a diverse ecosystem makes it difficult to ensure that all implementations remain equally robust, further complicating security efforts.

3.6 The Human Factor: Developer Missteps

3.6.1 Misconfigurations: How Simple Mistakes Lead to Major Vulnerabilities

One of the most common causes of security vulnerabilities is developer misconfigurations. With WebGPU, developers have more control over GPU operations than ever before, but this also means there are more opportunities to make critical mistakes. Misconfigured buffers, improper memory handling, or insecure shader code can open the door to attacks. A simple oversight, such as forgetting to sanitize inputs or failing to properly isolate GPU processes, can lead to severe security breaches. WebGPU's complexity increases the risk of these kinds of missteps, making developer education and best practices more important than ever.

3.6.2 Lack of Security Best Practices: What Developers Need to Know

Given the relative newness of WebGPU, many developers are not fully aware of the security risks it poses. Unlike more mature technologies like WebGL, WebGPU lacks a well-established set of best practices for securing applications. Many developers may focus on performance and overlook the security implications of their code. This lack of awareness can lead to insecure applications that are vulnerable to attacks. To address this, the WebGPU community needs to develop and promote clear, accessible security guidelines for developers, ensuring that security is baked into the development process from the beginning.

3.6.3 The Future of Secure WebGPU Development: Training and Awareness

For WebGPU to be secure, developers must be adequately trained on its complexities and potential pitfalls. As more web developers begin to adopt WebGPU, it's critical that they receive proper education on both its capabilities and its risks. Security-focused training should be a priority for any developer working with WebGPU, covering topics such as safe memory management, secure shader coding, and proper sandboxing techniques. Additionally, awareness campaigns highlighting common security pitfalls and their solutions will help foster a more security-conscious developer community.

3.7 Looking Ahead: Can WebGPU Be Secured?

3.7.1 The Current State of WebGPU Security: Progress and Setbacks

WebGPU is still in its infancy, and its security landscape is evolving rapidly. While some progress has been made, such as the implementation of basic security measures by browser vendors, there have also been setbacks. Vulnerabilities have already been identified and exploited, highlighting the need for continuous improvement in the API's security framework. As more developers and attackers explore WebGPU's capabilities, it is likely that new vulnerabilities will emerge, requiring ongoing vigilance and updates from both browser vendors and the developer community.

3.7.2 Potential Fixes: How WebGPU Could Be Made Safer

Several measures could be implemented to make WebGPU more secure. These include stronger sandboxing techniques, improved memory management tools, and more robust security testing frameworks. Additionally, browsers could enforce stricter policies around GPU access, ensuring that only trusted code can run low-level operations. Driver-level security enhancements from GPU manufacturers would also go a long way in closing potential attack vectors. While these fixes won't eliminate all risks, they would greatly reduce the likelihood of WebGPU being exploited by malicious actors.

3.8 Summary

WebGPU offers undeniable potential, but its security risks cannot be ignored. As with any powerful new technology, there is a trade-off between performance and security. While WebGPU can enable incredible advancements in web-based graphics and computation, it also opens up a wide range of new vulnerabilities. Whether the benefits of adopting WebGPU outweigh the risks will depend on how effectively the security challenges are addressed in the coming years. For now, developers must weigh these risks carefully before fully embracing the API.

4
Chapter

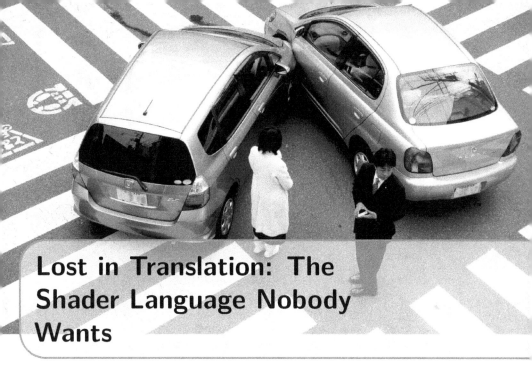

Lost in Translation: The Shader Language Nobody Wants

Quote: "Success is a lousy teacher. It seduces smart people into thinking they can't lose." (**Bill Gates**)

4.1 Introduction

WebGPU introduces a new shader language, WGSL (WebGPU Shading Language), which was designed to meet the unique needs of the API. However, many developers argue that this solution was unnecessary. Prior to WGSL, the web development community had successfully used GLSL (OpenGL Shading Language) or HLSL (High-Level Shading Language) to write shaders. These established languages had mature ecosystems, tooling, and widespread familiarity, allowing developers to create sophisticated graphics with minimal overhead. The introduction of WGSL seems to solve a problem that didn't really exist—adding complexity without delivering significant benefits over existing shader languages.

4.1.1 The Complexity Overload: Why Developers Are Struggling

WGSL, unlike GLSL or HLSL, introduces new syntax and concepts that can confuse even experienced developers. Instead of building on well-understood paradigms, WGSL brings additional complexity, including more rigid type systems and stricter requirements for memory management. While this added rigor may theoretically enhance performance and safety, in practice it creates a steep learning curve. Developers accustomed to more flexible shader languages find themselves overwhelmed by WGSL's strictness, turning what should be a streamlined process into a time-consuming and frustrating ordeal.

4.1.2 Fragmentation in the Shader Ecosystem: Compatibility Headaches

One of the most significant problems with introducing WGSL is the fragmentation it creates in the shader ecosystem. Developers who once could rely on their GLSL or HLSL code being portable across various APIs now face the challenge of managing codebases for multiple shading languages. This fragmentation leads to compatibility issues, as shaders written in WGSL cannot be easily ported to other graphics APIs without extensive rewriting. Instead of moving toward a unified standard, WebGPU's shader language has only exacerbated the divide, forcing developers to juggle multiple languages to maintain cross-platform compatibility.

4.2 Learning Curve and Developer Frustration

4.2.1 Too Much, Too Soon: The Steep Learning Curve of WebGPU Shaders

The introduction of WGSL places a heavy burden on developers, particularly those new to GPU programming. Learning any shader language can be challenging, but WGSL's additional complexities make it even more daunting. The language's emphasis on type safety and explicit memory management, while theoretically beneficial, can create significant barriers for developers. Instead of easing the transition into GPU programming, WGSL throws developers into the deep end, leaving many to grapple with its intricacies without sufficient guidance or support.

4.2.2 Lack of Familiarity: Why WebGPU Shaders Alienate Veteran Developers

Veteran developers who are well-versed in GLSL or HLSL often find WGSL alienating. Despite having years of experience in shader programming, many struggle with WGSL's different syntax and more rigid structure. Rather than building on the collective knowledge of existing shading languages, WGSL forces experienced developers to learn a new system from scratch, leading to frustration and resistance. This lack of continuity undermines one of the core strengths of the web development ecosystem—the ability to rapidly adopt new technologies without steep learning curves.

4.2.3 Missing Documentation: The Roadblocks to Learning the Language

A further complication with WGSL is the lack of comprehensive documentation. Many developers report that the existing WGSL documentation is sparse, inconsistent, or simply difficult to follow. Without clear examples or best practices, developers are left to decipher the language through trial and error. This lack of guidance makes an already challenging language even harder to learn, contributing to the growing frustration within the developer community. Until the documentation improves, WGSL will continue to alienate those trying to adopt it.

Food for Thought - Innovative Technologies That Fell Short: **Segway** (2001) - The Transport Revolution That Never Was - Touted as the future of personal transportation, the Segway was expensive and impractical for most. Its limited adoption and regulatory hurdles meant it never gained the mass appeal predicted.

4.3 Cross-Platform Discrepancies

4.3.1 Compatibility Nightmares: How WebGPU Shaders Behave Differently Across Platforms

One of the promises of WebGPU was cross-platform compatibility, but WGSL shaders often behave inconsistently across different browsers and hardware. Slight variations in how different platforms implement WebGPU mean that a shader which works perfectly on one device might fail on another. This variability creates significant headaches for developers, who now must test their shaders across a wider array of configurations to ensure consistent performance. The vision of a truly unified graphics API is undermined by these discrepancies, leading to a frustrating development experience.

4.3.2 Driver-Specific Issues: The Unspoken Challenge

Beyond the platform inconsistencies, driver-specific issues compound the problem. GPUs from different manufacturers handle shader code differently, leading to performance differences or even outright failures. These issues are often difficult to diagnose and resolve, as driver-level bugs can manifest in unpredictable ways. Developers who encounter these issues find themselves stuck in a cycle of debugging and testing, with little support from browser vendors or GPU manufacturers. This makes writing reliable, performant shaders a far more challenging task than it should be.

4.3.3 Why OpenGL Shaders Still Dominate: A Legacy That Won't Die

Despite the rise of WebGPU and WGSL, OpenGL shaders (GLSL) continue to dominate much of the web graphics landscape. GLSL's simplicity, widespread support, and extensive tooling make it the go-to choice for many developers, especially those targeting older or less powerful devices. The reluctance to abandon GLSL in favor of WGSL highlights the entrenched position that OpenGL shaders hold. Many developers see no reason to switch to WGSL, particularly given its added complexity and limited advantages over the well-established GLSL.

4.4 The Unrealized Promise of Flexibility

4.4.1 Promised Flexibility: What Was Expected from WebGPU's Shader Language

WGSL was marketed as a flexible, powerful shader language designed to meet the evolving needs of modern web applications. Proponents claimed that its type safety, memory control, and cross-platform design would make it a more versatile tool than GLSL or HLSL. However, for many developers, this promised flexibility has yet to materialize. Instead of simplifying shader development, WGSL has introduced new complexities, making it harder to achieve the performance and portability gains that were originally promised.

4.4.2 The Trade-Offs: Performance vs. Usability in Shader Design

One of the most significant trade-offs with WGSL is the balance between performance and usability. While the language's low-level control over memory and processing can theoretically lead to optimized performance, the complexity of managing these details often results in errors, inefficiency, and poor developer experiences. In practice, the effort required to achieve minor performance improvements may not justify the time and frustration spent wrestling with the language's intricacies. This trade-off leaves many questioning whether the gains are worth the cost in usability.

4.4.3 Failure to Standardize: How Fragmentation Slows Innovation

Despite WGSL's potential, its lack of widespread adoption and fragmentation within the shader language ecosystem are slowing innovation. By introducing yet another standard that competes with GLSL and HLSL, WebGPU has contributed to a fractured landscape where developers must choose between competing languages with no clear path forward. This fragmentation discourages developers from investing time in mastering WGSL, as its long-term viability remains uncertain. Instead of advancing web graphics, this failure to standardize has hindered progress and kept the industry mired in inefficiency.

4.5 Lack of Support in the Broader Ecosystem

4.5.1 The Industry Backlash: Why Developers Don't Want Another Shader Language

The introduction of WGSL has sparked backlash from many developers who feel that another shader language is unnecessary. The ecosystem already supports GLSL, HLSL, and other well-established languages, and the addition of WGSL adds complexity without offering enough unique advantages. Developers are resistant to adopting yet another language, particularly one that seems to have little support outside of WebGPU. This backlash has slowed WGSL's adoption and raised questions about its future relevance.

4.5.2 Limited Tooling: How Poor Support Hurts Development Efficiency

One of the most significant obstacles to WGSL's success is the lack of robust tooling. Existing shader development tools are primarily built around GLSL and HLSL, leaving WGSL with limited support in terms of debuggers, editors, and optimization tools. This lack of tooling hurts development efficiency, as developers are forced to build and debug WGSL shaders without the mature ecosystem that exists for other languages. Until this tooling gap is addressed, WGSL will continue to struggle in gaining widespread adoption.

4.5.3 Competing Standards: How Other APIs and Engines Handle Shaders Better

WebGPU's shader language also faces competition from other graphics APIs and engines that handle shaders more effectively. APIs like Vulkan and Metal offer more powerful, low-level access to hardware while maintaining compatibility with established shading languages. Meanwhile, popular game engines like Unity and Unreal Engine continue to rely on well-supported shader systems that are easier to learn and integrate. In comparison, WGSL feels like an outlier, offering little incentive for developers to move away from these more capable and familiar alternatives.

4.6 The Future of WebGPU Shaders

4.6.1 Can WebGPU Shaders Be Saved? The Push for Standardization

The future of WGSL is uncertain, but it's clear that for the language to succeed, it will need to overcome significant hurdles. One potential solution lies in greater standardization, both within WebGPU and across the broader graphics ecosystem. By aligning more closely with existing shader languages and tools, WGSL could become more appealing to developers. However, achieving this level of standardization will require collaboration between browser vendors, GPU manufacturers, and the developer community, a process that could take years.

4.6.2 The Road Ahead: Will WebGPU Shaders Evolve or Fade Away?

As WebGPU continues to develop, the fate of WGSL remains in question. Will the language evolve to meet the needs of the developer community, or will it be sidelined in favor of more familiar alternatives? Much will depend on whether browser vendors and industry leaders can address the language's current shortcomings. If they fail, WGSL risks becoming a relic—an unnecessary layer of complexity that developers avoid whenever possible.

4.7 Summary

In the end, WGSL represents a solution to a problem that didn't exist. While its goals of improving performance and safety are admirable, the reality is that developers simply didn't need another shader language. With GLSL and HLSL already meeting the needs of most developers, WGSL feels like an unnecessary burden. Unless significant changes are made, WGSL risks being remembered as a misstep—an ambitious but ultimately unwanted addition to the web graphics ecosystem.

5

Chapter

Robustness Failures: When WebGPU Breaks

Quote: "Innovation is the ability to see change as an opportunity – not a threat." (**Steve Jobs**)

5.1 Introduction

WebGPU entered the scene with promises of unmatched stability and performance, presenting itself as the next-generation graphics API for the web. The hype built around these claims has painted a picture of a seamless, robust platform that could handle anything thrown at it. However, as more developers have integrated WebGPU into real-world applications, cracks in the foundation have started to show. WebGPU, in reality, does not live up to these lofty promises. Rather than being the reliable API it was meant to be, WebGPU struggles with stability under complex, real-world loads, resulting in frequent failures and crashes.

5.1.1 Crashes and Instabilities: Why WebGPU Fails Under Pressure

Under controlled environments and small-scale projects, WebGPU might appear stable. But when pushed to the limit in larger applications or more demanding workloads, WebGPU often buckles under pressure. One reason for this instability is the sheer complexity of managing GPU resources across multiple platforms. Whether it's a game engine rendering intricate 3D scenes or scientific simulations that tax GPU memory, WebGPU can easily crash, often with little to no warning or useful error information. Developers face unreliable performance, where bugs only surface in production, making them harder to predict and fix.

5.1.2 Edge Cases: The Unexpected Ways WebGPU Breaks

The devil is in the details, and for WebGPU, edge cases have proven to be a nightmare. From handling uncommon hardware configurations to supporting outdated or lesser-known browsers, WebGPU's supposed flexibility breaks down. Small discrepancies in how different platforms handle memory allocation or GPU commands can lead to failures in applications that are otherwise stable. These edge cases make WebGPU a ticking time bomb for developers who need to account for a wide variety of user environments.

Food for Thought - Innovative Technologies That Fell Short: **Google Glass** (2013) - The Future of Augmented Reality – Just Too Soon - Google's foray into wearable AR was revolutionary, but high costs, privacy issues, and a lack of clear use cases doomed it before the world was ready to embrace the technology.

5.2 Driver Inconsistencies: A Weak Foundation

5.2.1 The Hidden Risks of GPU Drivers: Why They Matter More Than You Think

The performance and stability of WebGPU are inherently tied to the underlying GPU drivers. These drivers act as the bridge between the hardware and the API, and any weaknesses or inconsistencies in driver implementations can severely impact WebGPU's performance. Different manufacturers—whether it's NVIDIA, AMD, or Intel—have varying driver quality and implementation quirks. WebGPU's performance is at the mercy of these drivers, meaning that a robust, uniform experience is difficult to guarantee. GPU drivers are often updated at unpredictable intervals, adding another layer of instability to the mix.

5.2.2 Driver Variability: Different Hardware, Different Problems

WebGPU's cross-platform nature means it has to function well across a wide variety of hardware, from high-end GPUs to integrated graphics. This variability introduces a host of problems, as drivers for different hardware may implement features in divergent ways, or even lack support for certain WebGPU functions. A shader program that runs flawlessly on one GPU may crash on another, leading to inconsistent experiences for users. Even worse, some drivers are notorious for bugs that can corrupt memory or crash applications without warning, leaving developers scrambling to identify the root cause.

5.2.3 Browser Dependencies: How WebGPU's Stability Is Tied to the Browser

WebGPU's reliance on the browser as the delivery platform adds another layer of fragility. Browsers themselves are complex pieces of software that must manage numerous APIs, of which WebGPU is just one. Variations in how different browsers—such as Chrome, Firefox, or Safari—handle WebGPU commands mean that applications can behave inconsistently across platforms. Furthermore, browser updates can inadvertently break WebGPU functionality, causing crashes or performance issues that are beyond the control of developers. This dependency on browser behavior makes WebGPU a less stable choice for critical applications.

5.3 Resource Management Issues

5.3.1 Memory Leaks: WebGPU's Silent Performance Killers

Memory leaks in WebGPU applications represent one of the most silent yet damaging robustness failures. A memory leak occurs when an application continuously allocates memory without properly releasing it, eventually exhausting available system resources. In WebGPU, managing GPU memory efficiently is crucial, but the API provides minimal safeguards to prevent developers from introducing leaks. Over time, these leaks degrade performance, and in severe cases, they can cause entire systems to crash. This issue becomes particularly apparent in long-running applications or services that require extensive use of the GPU, such as streaming platforms or simulations.

5.3.2 Resource Exhaustion: When WebGPU Overloads Your System

Beyond memory leaks, WebGPU can easily overload system resources if not properly managed. GPU memory, in particular, is a finite resource, and when WebGPU attempts to allocate more than the hardware can handle, the results can be catastrophic. Resource exhaustion often leads to system instability, freezing, or even forced shutdowns. The lack of clear error reporting during resource-intensive operations means developers often don't know they're on the verge of crashing the system until it's too late. This makes WebGPU a risky choice for applications that push the boundaries of what modern hardware can handle.

5.3.3 Poor Resource Cleanup: How WebGPU Leaves Systems Vulnerable

One of WebGPU's biggest weaknesses lies in its failure to enforce proper resource cleanup. After GPU resources—such as buffers, textures, or shaders—are no longer needed, they must be explicitly released by the developer. Failure to do so can leave orphaned resources consuming precious system memory. In time, these leftovers accumulate, leading to degraded system performance. Worse, they can act as a gateway for malicious attacks, as unmanaged resources provide an opportunity for exploitation. The burden of managing these resources is entirely on the developer, creating ample room for mistakes.

5.4 Concurrency Problems: Multi-Threading Gone Wrong

5.4.1 Race Conditions: The Hidden Danger of Parallel Processing

Concurrency in WebGPU allows for parallel processing, enabling faster performance by distributing tasks across multiple threads. However, with this power comes the risk of race conditions, where two or more threads access shared resources simultaneously. If a race condition occurs, it can corrupt data or cause unpredictable application behavior. WebGPU does little to guard against such issues, leaving developers to implement their own safeguards. In complex applications, these race conditions can remain hidden until the application is scaled up, leading to devastating crashes at the most inopportune times.

5.4.2 Synchronization Failures: Why WebGPU Struggles with Concurrency

Synchronization failures occur when parallel tasks are not correctly managed, leading to out-of-order execution or incomplete operations. WebGPU's multi-threaded architecture, while designed to boost performance, often struggles with proper synchronization, especially when dealing with complex rendering pipelines. Poor synchronization can result in graphical glitches, corrupted data, or entire processes hanging indefinitely. Debugging such issues is notoriously difficult, as they may only surface intermittently, depending on the timing and order of operations.

5.4.3 Performance vs. Stability: How WebGPU Sacrifices Robustness for Speed

In the pursuit of speed, WebGPU often sacrifices stability. The ability to run multiple tasks concurrently can improve performance, but it also increases the likelihood of errors that compromise robustness. Developers frequently have to choose between optimizing for performance or ensuring the stability of their applications, as WebGPU's tools for managing concurrency are insufficient for guaranteeing both. As a result, applications that aim for high-performance often end up riddled with bugs and instability.

5.5 Debugging Nightmares: When Things Go Wrong

5.5.1 Lack of Diagnostic Tools: Why WebGPU Is Hard to Debug

One of the most significant challenges developers face with WebGPU is the lack of comprehensive diagnostic tools. When something goes wrong—whether it's a crash, performance issue, or rendering error—the API provides minimal insight into what caused the problem. Traditional debugging tools used for WebGL or other APIs are either non-existent or poorly integrated with WebGPU. As a result, developers are left to guess the source of the problem, wasting valuable time trying to track down bugs without sufficient information.

5.5.2 Cryptic Error Messages: When WebGPU Leaves Developers in the Dark

Even when WebGPU does provide error messages, they are often cryptic and unhelpful. Instead of offering clear guidance on what went wrong, error messages might be vague or overly technical, leaving developers struggling to interpret their meaning. For example, an error like "Out of memory" could be the result of numerous underlying issues—anything from inefficient resource management to driver problems. This lack of transparency makes fixing bugs a frustrating and time-consuming process, deterring many developers from fully embracing WebGPU.

5.5.3 Real-World Debugging Challenges: Examples from the Field

Real-world examples of debugging WebGPU applications show just how challenging the process can be. For instance, developers working on complex 3D games have reported intermittent crashes that only occur on specific hardware configurations, making it nearly impossible to reproduce the issue consistently. In other cases, GPU-related errors only manifest after the application has been running for several hours, further complicating the debugging process. These real-world challenges highlight the need for better diagnostic tools and clearer error messaging to make WebGPU a more reliable platform for developers.

5.6 Platform-Specific Failures

5.6.1 Windows Woes: WebGPU's Problems on the Most Popular OS

Despite Windows being the dominant platform for many developers and users, WebGPU has encountered numerous issues specific to this operating system. Driver inconsistencies, resource management problems, and compatibility issues with different GPU vendors have all contributed to WebGPU's instability on Windows. As a result, developers often find that their applications perform well on other platforms but experience random crashes or degraded performance on Windows. This platform-specific instability makes developing cross-platform applications with WebGPU even more challenging.

5.6.2 macOS and Metal: Compatibility Issues and Failures

WebGPU's integration with macOS relies on Apple's Metal API, and this introduces a host of unique problems. While Metal is a powerful graphics API, its implementation can differ significantly from other platforms like DirectX or Vulkan, leading to compatibility issues for WebGPU. For example, certain WebGPU features may not be fully supported on Metal, causing crashes or degraded performance in applications. Developers must spend additional time tailoring their applications to ensure compatibility, and even then, Metal-specific bugs can still arise.

5.6.3 Linux and Open-Source: When WebGPU Collides with Non-Proprietary Systems

Linux, known for its open-source ecosystem, presents its own set of challenges for WebGPU. The fragmented nature of the Linux platform, with multiple distributions and varying GPU driver support, makes achieving consistent performance difficult. Furthermore, open-source drivers for GPUs often lag behind their proprietary counterparts in terms of stability and feature support, leading to crashes and poor performance when running WebGPU applications. This issue is further exacerbated by the lack of dedicated support from major hardware vendors for the Linux platform, leaving developers with few options for reliable GPU performance.

5.7 Recovering from Failures: How Resilient Is WebGPU?

5.7.1 Error Handling: Why WebGPU Struggles to Recover from Crashes

One of the most glaring weaknesses of WebGPU is its inability to recover gracefully from errors. When an application encounters a crash or instability, WebGPU lacks robust error-handling mechanisms to recover or mitigate the impact. Often, a crash results in the entire application freezing or shutting down, forcing users to restart the process. This lack of resilience makes WebGPU unsuitable for mission-critical applications that require continuous uptime, as even minor errors can result in complete application failure.

5.7.2 Automatic Recovery: Does WebGPU Offer Robust Fallbacks?

In the realm of graphics APIs, automatic recovery mechanisms are essential for maintaining application stability. However, WebGPU offers limited options for fallback behavior when something goes wrong. For instance, if a shader compilation fails or a GPU resource is exhausted, WebGPU provides no built-in methods for gracefully degrading performance or switching to an alternative configuration. This lack of fallback options leaves developers with the arduous task of implementing their own recovery systems, adding complexity to the development process and increasing the likelihood of bugs.

5.7.3 Long-Term Stability: Is WebGPU Ready for Large-Scale Applications?

Given the numerous robustness issues, it's clear that WebGPU is not yet ready for large-scale, long-term applications. Memory leaks, resource management failures, and concurrency problems make WebGPU a risky choice for projects that require long-term stability. Until the API matures and resolves these fundamental issues, developers will continue to struggle with maintaining performance and reliability over extended periods of time.

5.8 Summary

Despite its promise, WebGPU's robustness failures highlight a significant gap between its potential and its current reality. The API has numerous weaknesses, from resource management issues to platform-specific failures, that make it unreliable for developers looking to build stable, high-performance applications. Until these issues are addressed, WebGPU will remain a tool with untapped potential, but one that is difficult to rely on in practice.

There are valuable lessons to be learned from WebGPU's robustness failures. First, the need for better cross-platform compatibility is crucial. WebGPU's reliance on drivers and platform-specific implementations makes it inherently fragile. Second, developers require more robust diagnostic tools and error-handling mechanisms to identify and recover from issues. Without these improvements, WebGPU's promise will remain unfulfilled.

For WebGPU to truly become a reliable, robust platform, several key changes must be made. Improved error handling, better diagnostic tools, and more consistent driver support across platforms are essential. Moreover, the development community must push for better standards and collaboration between hardware vendors, browser developers, and API maintainers. Only then will WebGPU reach its full potential and become the stable graphics API it was meant to be.

6

Chapter

The Compatibility Conundrum: Unsupported Everywhere

Quote: "Our technology has surpassed our humanity." (**Albert Einstein**)

6.1 Introduction

WebGPU was envisioned as a cross-platform solution, capable of running seamlessly on any device. However, in practice, this promise remains largely unfulfilled. Despite efforts to ensure wide compatibility, many platforms either lack full support for WebGPU or present major implementation inconsistencies. Developers find themselves caught between different hardware and browser environments, each introducing its own challenges, leading to the realization that WebGPU is not the universal API it claims to be.

6.1.1 Partial Support: Platforms That Haven't Fully Embraced WebGPU

Although WebGPU has gained traction in some browsers and operating systems, many major platforms either provide partial support or none at all. Browsers such as Safari lag behind in

WebGPU adoption, and operating systems like iOS present significant challenges due to limited GPU access. This incomplete platform support creates significant barriers for developers trying to build cross-platform applications. Furthermore, the inconsistent implementation of WebGPU features across these platforms leads to fragmented experiences for users.

6.1.2 The Mobile Gap: Why WebGPU Struggles on Phones and Tablets

Mobile devices, which have become the primary computing platform for millions of users, pose significant challenges for WebGPU. Performance constraints, limited GPU power, and lack of uniform driver support across Android and iOS make WebGPU's promise of compatibility difficult to achieve. On mobile, WebGPU frequently encounters performance bottlenecks or crashes due to resource limitations, rendering it almost unusable for graphics-heavy applications like games or simulations. The lack of proper support on mobile effectively undermines WebGPU's claim to be a truly cross-device solution.

6.2 Inconsistent Browser Support

6.2.1 Different Standards: Why WebGPU Varies Between Browsers

WebGPU's implementation varies considerably between browsers, leading to frustrating incompatibilities for developers. While Chrome and Firefox have taken the lead in supporting WebGPU, other browsers like Safari are lagging behind or have different levels of feature support. These discrepancies result in inconsistent behavior across browsers, making it difficult for developers to write code that works seamlessly on all platforms. The differences in WebGPU's implementation and standards result in developers needing to write browser-specific code, reintroducing a problem that modern web development sought to avoid.

6.2.2 Experimental Flags: Hidden Features and Incomplete Support

In many browsers, WebGPU remains an experimental feature that must be manually enabled by the user through specific flags. This hidden, incomplete support is a barrier for mainstream adoption, as end users are often unaware or unwilling to enable these experimental features. Developers, too, are reluctant to build applications on top of features that require users to take additional steps to enable functionality. The reliance on experimental flags shows that WebGPU is not yet ready for widespread use.

6.2.3 Deprecation of WebGL: Can WebGPU Fill the Void?

As WebGL, the longstanding web graphics API, is slowly being phased out, WebGPU is positioned as its successor. However, the transition has been anything but smooth. Many platforms that fully support WebGL either lack full WebGPU compatibility or have substantial differences in performance and feature sets. Until WebGPU reaches the same level of maturity as WebGL, developers are reluctant to move their applications over. This has created an awkward in-between phase where neither WebGL nor WebGPU is an ideal solution, leaving developers in a bind.

Food for Thought - Innovative Technologies That Fell Short: **Apple Newton** (1993) - A Groundbreaking PDA with Fatal Flaws - Apple's Newton was ahead of its time as a personal digital assistant, but its hefty price and unreliable handwriting recognition caused it to flop, despite being a precursor to today's smartphones.

6.3 Hardware Limitations

6.3.1 GPU Support: The Wide Variety of GPU Architectures

One of WebGPU's key challenges is supporting the wide variety of GPU architectures available today. High-end GPUs, integrated graphics, and mobile GPUs all handle WebGPU's commands differently, introducing a host of compatibility problems. For instance, shader code optimized for a high-end desktop GPU may perform poorly or not at all on integrated or mobile graphics. This variation in GPU capabilities and support undermines WebGPU's claim to provide a unified development experience.

6.3.2 Legacy Hardware: When Old GPUs Can't Keep Up

Another significant issue with WebGPU compatibility is legacy hardware support. Many older devices still in use today lack the hardware capabilities required to fully utilize WebGPU's features, leading to either degraded performance or outright incompatibility. Users with older graphics cards or integrated GPUs may find that WebGPU-based applications run slowly, crash, or fail to load entirely. This creates a significant challenge for developers who need to decide whether to optimize for modern hardware or support older devices.

6.3.3 Vendor-Specific Optimizations: How NVIDIA, AMD, and Intel Vary

Even among modern GPUs, differences between vendors such as NVIDIA, AMD, and Intel create unique compatibility challenges for WebGPU. Each vendor offers different optimizations, capabilities, and driver support, leading to variations in how WebGPU performs. Developers often need to implement vendor-specific optimizations to ensure that their applications run smoothly across a range of hardware, increasing development complexity and eroding WebGPU's promise of a universal API.

6.4 OS-Specific Issues

6.4.1 Windows and DirectX: A Challenging Relationship

WebGPU's integration with Windows often leads to compatibility challenges due to the dominance of DirectX, Microsoft's proprietary graphics API. DirectX is deeply integrated into the Windows operating system, and this tight coupling sometimes complicates WebGPU's functionality, especially when dealing with DirectX-specific features or optimizations. As a result, WebGPU applications may not run as efficiently on Windows as those built directly using DirectX, leading developers to question whether WebGPU is the best option for Windows-based projects.

6.4.2 macOS and Metal: A Layer of Complexity

On macOS, WebGPU relies on Apple's Metal API for graphics rendering, which introduces an additional layer of complexity. While Metal is a powerful API, its unique architecture differs from Vulkan or DirectX, requiring WebGPU to adapt to a different set of graphics commands. This can result in performance issues or incompatibilities, particularly for developers who are accustomed to working with Vulkan or DirectX. The result is that WebGPU on macOS may not perform as well as it does on other platforms, creating yet another compatibility headache for developers.

6.4.3 Linux and Vulkan: Fragmentation in the Open-Source World

Linux presents its own set of challenges for WebGPU, as the platform's reliance on open-source drivers and the Vulkan API creates a fragmented development environment. Not all Linux distributions fully support Vulkan, and driver support can vary significantly between distributions and GPU vendors. This fragmentation leads to inconsistent WebGPU performance and compatibility across Linux systems. For developers targeting Linux, this means additional testing and optimization are required, further complicating cross-platform development.

6.5 Development Environment Woes

6.5.1 Tooling Gaps: Limited Support from IDEs and Debuggers

WebGPU's tooling ecosystem remains immature compared to more established APIs like WebGL or DirectX. Popular integrated development environments (IDEs) and debugging tools often lack comprehensive support for WebGPU, making it difficult for developers to debug, profile, and optimize their applications. This lack of robust tooling slows down development and increases the risk of bugs slipping into production, deterring many developers from adopting WebGPU in the first place.

6.5.2 Shader Development Challenges: Language Barriers and Debugging

Developing shaders for WebGPU introduces additional challenges, particularly when dealing with the specific shader languages WebGPU requires. These languages, such as WGSL (WebGPU Shading Language), differ from more familiar shader languages like GLSL or HLSL, which creates a learning curve for developers. Furthermore, debugging shaders in WebGPU is often more difficult due to the lack of mature tools, making shader development a frustrating experience for many.

6.5.3 Lack of Integration with Popular Engines: Unreal, Unity, and Others

Many developers rely on game engines like Unreal Engine and Unity to build complex applications. However, WebGPU has yet to be fully integrated into these engines, meaning that developers must either work with less mature WebGPU integrations or stick with the older WebGL or proprietary APIs. The lack of out-of-the-box support for WebGPU in these widely-used engines significantly hampers adoption and limits the types of projects that can realistically be built using WebGPU.

6.6 Looking Forward: Can WebGPU Overcome Compatibility Issues?

6.6.1 The Path to Wider Support: What Needs to Happen?

For WebGPU to truly succeed as a cross-platform graphics API, significant improvements are needed in terms of platform support, browser compatibility, and hardware optimization. Collaboration between browser vendors, hardware manufacturers, and API developers will be key to ensuring a more consistent and reliable WebGPU experience. Furthermore, improving the API's performance on mobile devices and legacy hardware is crucial for widespread adoption.

6.6.2 Standardization Efforts: Can WebGPU Become a Universal API?

Efforts are underway to standardize WebGPU across platforms and browsers, but significant challenges remain. For WebGPU to fulfill its promise of being a universal API, it must overcome the fragmented landscape of GPU architectures, operating systems, and browsers. The development community must push for stricter adherence to standards and better collaboration across the various platforms WebGPU is intended to support.

6.7 Summary

While WebGPU holds the potential to be the next-generation web graphics API, the current state of compatibility issues across platforms, hardware, and browsers suggests that this dream is still far from being fully realized. Without significant progress in these areas, developers will continue to face challenges in delivering consistent, high-performance applications using WebGPU. Whether WebGPU can overcome these hurdles remains to be seen, but for now, the promise of universal compatibility remains just that—a promise.

7
Chapter

API Chaos: Too Many Cooks in the Kitchen

Quote: "Technology is nothing. What's important is that you have a faith in people, that they're good and smart, and if you give them tools, they'll do wonderful things with them." (**Steve Jobs**)

7.1 Introduction

Over the past several decades, the number of graphics APIs has exploded. What began with foundational technologies like OpenGL and DirectX has now expanded to include Vulkan, Metal, and WebGPU, among others. Each new API emerged to address specific limitations of its predecessors, but rather than streamlining development, this proliferation has led to fragmentation. Multiple vendors and platforms push their own standards, and developers find themselves caught between competing approaches, each with different learning curves, support structures, and performance promises. As a result, what was once a fairly unified landscape has become a crowded field of competing technologies, each claiming to offer something better but collectively overwhelming the development community.

7.1.1 Redundancy or Evolution? Why New APIs Keep Emerging

Every new API promises revolutionary features or better performance than its predecessors, but how much of this is truly necessary? Developers often ask whether these APIs represent genuine technological evolution or simply redundant options that create more work without significant benefits. For instance, Vulkan was hailed as a more modern and efficient successor to OpenGL, offering greater control over hardware, but its complexity is often overkill for simpler applications. Similarly, Apple's Metal provided optimized performance for macOS and iOS but fractured the ecosystem further by locking developers into proprietary tools. This section explores whether new APIs actually push the boundaries of technology or merely multiply the complexity without providing substantial advantages.

7.1.2 Fragmentation vs. Innovation: The Balance Between Choice and Chaos

There's a fine line between offering developers choices and overwhelming them with too many options. While competition can spur innovation, too much fragmentation can paralyze progress. A crowded API landscape forces developers to choose which platforms and technologies to prioritize, but this decision is rarely straightforward. Cross-platform development becomes an exercise in compromise, where the optimal performance on one platform could lead to significant degradation on another. While innovation is essential to move the industry forward, the chaotic state of APIs today suggests that the balance between offering diverse tools and creating a unified standard is tipping in the wrong direction.

7.2 Vendor Wars: Competing Standards, Competing Agendas

7.2.1 NVIDIA, AMD, and Intel: The Battle for API Supremacy

Graphics API chaos is fueled, in large part, by competition among GPU vendors. NVIDIA, AMD, and Intel each have their own vested interests in supporting certain APIs, whether it's NVIDIA's push for CUDA and Vulkan, AMD's historical backing of Mantle, or Intel's preference for open standards like OpenCL. These competing agendas mean that developers often have to tailor their applications to specific hardware to take full advantage of the GPU's power. While this competition can drive technological progress, it also splinters the development process, forcing developers to write multiple code paths or optimize for specific GPUs, thus complicating cross-platform compatibility.

7.2.2 Platform Lock-In: How Proprietary APIs Fuel Fragmentation

Proprietary APIs like Microsoft's DirectX and Apple's Metal exacerbate the fragmentation problem by limiting flexibility for developers. DirectX has long been tied to Windows, offering significant performance advantages on the platform but forcing developers to adopt separate strategies for other systems. Similarly, Metal, while optimized for Apple devices, has little utility outside of the macOS and iOS ecosystems. These proprietary APIs prioritize vendor control over ecosystem interoperability, locking developers into specific hardware and software environments. As a result, developers must juggle different APIs for different platforms, further contributing to the API chaos.

7.2.3 The Open Standard Dilemma: Is Vulkan the Solution or Part of the Problem?

Vulkan was introduced as an open standard to address the very issues caused by API fragmentation, promising a unified solution for high-performance graphics across different platforms. However, while Vulkan provides developers with fine-grained control over GPU resources, it also introduces a steep learning curve. For many developers, the complexity of Vulkan outweighs its benefits, especially for simpler applications. Additionally, support for Vulkan across devices and drivers remains inconsistent, making it another piece in the growing puzzle rather than a comprehensive solution. The question remains: can Vulkan truly unify the API landscape, or is it just another API adding to the chaos?

Food for Thought - Innovative Technologies That Fell Short: **BlackBerry PlayBook** (2011) - A Tablet Without the Basics - BlackBerry's attempt to compete with the iPad missed the mark by shipping without crucial features like email or calendar apps. Combined with BlackBerry's declining market presence, it was a failure.

7.3 WebGPU's Role in the Chaos

7.3.1 A Unified Standard or Just Another API?

WebGPU was heralded as the answer to cross-platform web-based graphics, designed to unify the fragmented space that WebGL could no longer sufficiently serve. However, in practice, it has added another layer of complexity. WebGPU offers developers a new set of tools but doesn't always integrate smoothly with other established APIs. This has led many to question whether WebGPU simplifies the development process or whether it simply becomes yet another API to learn, with its own quirks and limitations. Instead of bringing harmony to the web graphics world, WebGPU may have contributed to the ever-growing confusion in the API space.

7.3.2 The Lack of Interoperability: WebGPU's Struggle to Integrate with Existing APIs

Despite its intentions, WebGPU often struggles to coexist with other graphics APIs. Developers trying to integrate WebGPU with systems that rely on Vulkan, DirectX, or OpenGL frequently encounter compatibility issues. These hurdles stem from differences in how each API handles resources, shaders, and device interactions. Developers face additional overhead when writing compatibility layers or workarounds, detracting from the intended benefits of adopting WebGPU. This lack of interoperability complicates projects, especially for developers who hoped WebGPU would be the "one API to rule them all."

7.3.3 Is WebGPU Really Necessary? Analyzing the Justification for Its Existence

The introduction of WebGPU has raised the question of whether the industry really needed another graphics API. WebGL, while aging, still serves many use cases, and newer APIs like Vulkan are already addressing high-performance needs. This section critically examines whether WebGPU offers significant advantages that justify its existence or if it was created in response to industry hype rather than actual developer demand. With its complexity and interoperability issues, WebGPU's necessity remains debatable, especially considering the already vast array of APIs that developers must navigate.

7.4 The Developer's Dilemma: Too Many APIs, Too Little Time

7.4.1 Learning Curve Fatigue: Why Developers Are Overwhelmed

Developers today are inundated with new APIs, each requiring a different set of skills and knowledge. WebGPU, Vulkan, DirectX,

OpenGL, and Metal all have their own unique architectures, meaning developers often need to learn multiple systems to work across platforms. This steep learning curve is a significant barrier to entry, particularly for smaller teams or independent developers who lack the resources to specialize in every API. As more APIs enter the ecosystem, the time and energy spent learning and mastering them continue to grow, leaving many developers overwhelmed.

7.4.2 Maintaining Legacy Code: The Challenges of Supporting Multiple APIs

One of the most significant challenges developers face is the need to maintain legacy codebases that use older APIs like OpenGL or DirectX 11 while also adapting to newer technologies. The effort required to maintain compatibility across multiple APIs can significantly slow development cycles and increase costs. For example, a game originally built using OpenGL might require extensive reworking to support Vulkan or WebGPU. This necessity to juggle both old and new APIs creates logistical nightmares for development teams, especially when technical debt accumulates from maintaining outdated code while trying to integrate newer solutions.

7.4.3 Cross-Platform Complications: Writing Once, Running Nowhere?

The promise of writing code once and running it anywhere has been a long-standing dream in the development world, but with the fragmentation of APIs, this goal remains elusive. Despite the availability of cross-platform frameworks, developers still face significant challenges in ensuring their applications behave consistently across different operating systems and hardware. APIs like WebGPU, Vulkan, and DirectX each have their own platform-specific quirks, meaning developers often need to write custom solutions for each platform to ensure consistent performance. Far from achieving the goal of "write once, run anywhere," today's API chaos has resulted in "write once, fix everywhere."

7.5 Tooling and Documentation: A Mess of Inconsistencies

7.5.1 Inconsistent Documentation: When API Specs Leave Developers Guessing

One of the most frustrating aspects of dealing with multiple APIs is the inconsistency in their documentation. While some APIs, such as DirectX, come with extensive and well-organized documentation, others, like WebGPU, are still evolving, leaving developers to piece together information from incomplete or outdated resources. This lack of consistent, comprehensive documentation not only slows down the development process but also increases the risk of errors as developers are forced to make assumptions or experiment to understand how certain API functions work.

7.5.2 Fragmented Tooling: Why Debugging Across APIs Is a Nightmare

Debugging applications that rely on multiple graphics APIs is a complicated task. Each API has its own set of debugging and profiling tools, which are often incompatible with one another. For example, a developer might use NVIDIA's Nsight for debugging Vulkan code but need entirely different tools when working with WebGPU or Metal. This fragmentation in tooling creates inefficiencies, as developers must learn and switch between different debugging environments depending on the API they are working with. The lack of cohesive, cross-API tooling adds yet another layer of complexity to an already chaotic ecosystem.

7.5.3 The Lack of Standardization in Development Environments

The fragmentation of APIs extends beyond the graphics pipeline into the broader development environment. Different APIs require different integrated development environments (IDEs), compilers, and build tools. For example, a developer might use Microsoft Visual Studio for DirectX but switch to Xcode for Metal development on macOS. This lack of standardization complicates the development process, as it forces teams to manage multiple toolchains, which can lead to inconsistencies in code quality, performance, and debugging capabilities. Without a standardized development environment, the API chaos continues to proliferate.

7.6 Looking for Solutions: Can the API Chaos Be Tamed?

7.6.1 Unified Abstractions: Is It Time for a Meta-API?

One potential solution to the current API chaos is the development of a meta-API—a single abstraction layer that could interface with multiple graphics APIs. A meta-API would allow developers to write code once and have it translated into the appropriate calls for Vulkan, WebGPU, Metal, and other APIs, reducing the need for platform-specific code. While this idea is appealing, creating such an abstraction is fraught with challenges, particularly when it comes to performance. Abstraction layers can introduce overhead, reducing the fine-grained control that many developers rely on. Still, the prospect of a meta-API offers a possible path toward reducing the fragmentation in today's API landscape.

7.6.2 Industry Collaboration: A Path to Standardization?

The current fragmentation of graphics APIs is largely driven by competition between major companies like Microsoft, Apple, Google, and NVIDIA. If these companies were to collaborate on a unified API standard, much of the chaos could be alleviated. However, the likelihood of such collaboration remains low, given the conflicting interests and competitive advantages each company seeks to maintain. Nonetheless, increased industry collaboration, particularly around open standards like Vulkan, could pave the way for a more streamlined and unified API ecosystem. Standardization efforts, while difficult, offer a potential solution to the growing complexity faced by developers.

7.7 Summary

As the number of graphics APIs continues to grow, developers are increasingly caught in the crossfire of competing standards, platforms, and tools. While APIs like Vulkan, WebGPU, and Metal each offer distinct advantages, the overall landscape is more fragmented than ever, making it difficult for developers to deliver cross-platform solutions efficiently. Looking forward, the key to taming this chaos may lie in developing better abstractions, improving collaboration between vendors, and standardizing development tools. Until then, developers will continue to face the challenges of navigating an increasingly chaotic API ecosystem.

8

Chapter

Why Performance Falls Short of Expectations

Quote: "The greatest glory in living lies not in never falling, but in rising every time we fall." (**Nelson Mandela**)

8.1 Introduction

When WebGPU was first introduced, it was hailed as the next big leap in web graphics, promising unparalleled performance improvements over WebGL. The potential to access GPU power directly from the browser opened the door to fast, efficient rendering, complex simulations, and high-end game graphics, all without the need for native applications. Marketing around WebGPU focused on its ability to streamline performance bottlenecks and take full advantage of modern hardware. However, the reality for many developers is quite different. While WebGPU provides more control over the GPU, the expected performance boosts have not been universally realized. Many factors—including browser overhead, driver inconsistencies, and cross-platform support—have caused the performance gains to fall short of initial promises.

8.1.1 Bottlenecks in the Pipeline: Where Performance Breaks Down

One of the biggest misconceptions about WebGPU is that it eliminates the performance bottlenecks that plagued previous APIs like WebGL. However, performance is not simply a matter of GPU access; it is about how efficiently data flows through the entire pipeline. WebGPU's design introduces complexities in command processing, memory management, and synchronization that, in many cases, create new bottlenecks. For instance, moving data between the CPU and GPU can still be slow, particularly when handling large datasets or real-time applications. These bottlenecks become especially problematic when developers attempt to push WebGPU to its limits, often leading to underwhelming performance results.

8.1.2 The Optimization Illusion: Why Tuning WebGPU Isn't Enough

Optimization in WebGPU is often presented as the silver bullet for performance issues. However, even highly optimized WebGPU code may struggle to achieve the desired results. This is due to the inherent limitations of the API's design. While WebGPU allows for lower-level access to the GPU, this control requires developers to manage more aspects of the rendering process manually, increasing the likelihood of inefficiencies. Additionally, performance is often constrained by the environment in which WebGPU runs— whether it be browser overhead, varying hardware configurations, or the underlying operating system. In this sense, the belief that optimization alone can solve WebGPU's performance problems is largely an illusion.

> **Food for Thought** - Innovative Technologies That Fell Short: **Google Wave** (2009) - A Brilliant Idea that Was Just Too Complicated - Google Wave aimed to redefine communication and collaboration, but its overly complex interface and unclear purpose left users confused, and it quickly faded into obscurity.

8.2 Hardware Limitations: The GPU Isn't Always the Problem

8.2.1 The CPU-GPU Balance: Why CPU Bottlenecks Impact WebGPU

Despite WebGPU's focus on leveraging GPU power, the performance of web applications often hinges on how efficiently the CPU can communicate with the GPU. For instance, even if WebGPU makes better use of the GPU's capabilities, a weak or overburdened CPU can bottleneck the process, leading to suboptimal performance. Tasks such as handling input/output operations, preparing data for the GPU, and managing threads all depend heavily on the CPU. Therefore, the CPU-GPU balance remains a critical factor in determining overall performance. Even the most powerful GPU cannot compensate for a bottlenecked CPU.

8.2.2 Legacy Hardware: How Older Systems Struggle with WebGPU

While WebGPU promises to utilize modern GPU features effectively, legacy hardware often struggles to keep pace. Many users still run older GPUs that lack the necessary support for advanced features like parallel compute shaders or efficient memory management. WebGPU may attempt to scale down or emulate features for these older systems, but this can lead to significant performance degradation. In essence, WebGPU's full potential can only be realized on modern hardware, leaving users with outdated systems behind.

8.2.3 Power Consumption and Thermal Throttling: Hidden Performance Costs

WebGPU's ability to push hardware to its limits also comes with hidden costs—particularly in power consumption and heat generation. High-performance rendering can lead to significant energy consumption, causing devices to overheat. When temperatures rise too high, most systems will throttle performance to prevent damage, further reducing WebGPU's real-world performance. This is particularly problematic for laptops and mobile devices, where power efficiency and thermal management are critical. While WebGPU may theoretically unlock greater performance, the practical limitations of power consumption and heat dissipation often cap what can be achieved.

8.3 API Overhead: When Abstraction Hurts Performance

8.3.1 The Price of Abstraction: WebGPU vs. Native APIs

One of the key trade-offs in using WebGPU is the overhead introduced by its abstraction layer. Unlike native APIs like Vulkan or Metal, which offer direct low-level access to the GPU, WebGPU adds an extra layer of abstraction to ensure it works across different platforms and browsers. This abstraction is designed to make the API more accessible to developers, but it comes at a cost: performance. The additional processing required to abstract hardware-specific details results in overhead that native APIs do not have. This often means that applications running on WebGPU will perform slower compared to those using platform-specific APIs.

8.3.2 Cross-Platform Penalties: How Supporting Multiple Platforms Slows Everything Down

WebGPU's goal of being a cross-platform API necessitates compromises in how it interacts with different systems. Each platform—be it Windows, macOS, or Linux—has its own way of handling GPU resources, memory, and threading. To ensure that WebGPU works seamlessly across all these environments, developers must implement compatibility layers that introduce delays and inefficiencies. These layers, while necessary for WebGPU's mission of universal support, slow down performance by adding additional steps in the rendering pipeline. As a result, the performance of WebGPU often lags behind native APIs that are optimized for specific hardware and operating systems.

8.3.3 Memory Management Failures: Inefficiencies in WebGPU's Handling of Resources

Another critical area where WebGPU's abstraction creates performance problems is memory management. Native APIs provide fine-grained control over memory allocation and deallocation, allowing developers to optimize resource usage for maximum efficiency. In contrast, WebGPU's abstraction layer limits this control, often leading to inefficient memory usage. Poor memory management can result in memory leaks, fragmented memory pools, and overall slower performance, particularly in memory-intensive applications such as 3D rendering and large-scale simulations. These inefficiencies can significantly impact WebGPU's ability to maintain high performance over extended periods of use.

8.4 The Challenge of Real-World Performance

8.4.1 Benchmarking Deception: Why Lab Tests Don't Match Real-World Results

Lab-based benchmarks often paint a rosy picture of WebGPU's capabilities, but they rarely reflect the challenges of real-world applications. Benchmark tests typically run in controlled environments with optimized code and minimal interference from background processes, leading to inflated performance metrics. However, when WebGPU is deployed in the wild—on systems with varying hardware, running multiple applications simultaneously—performance tends to suffer. Factors such as network latency, browser load, and hardware inconsistencies make real-world performance far more unpredictable and less impressive than benchmark results suggest.

8.4.2 Application Complexity: How Large Projects Expose WebGPU's Weaknesses

While WebGPU can handle simple applications fairly well, its performance struggles become evident in more complex projects. Large-scale applications, such as AAA games or sophisticated scientific simulations, push WebGPU's architecture to its limits. These projects demand efficient memory management, high concurrency, and stable synchronization between threads—areas where WebGPU is notoriously weak. As the complexity of the application grows, so do the performance issues, with many developers reporting that WebGPU fails to keep pace with the demands of their larger projects.

8.4.3 Real-Time Graphics: Why WebGPU Struggles with Intensive Workloads

Real-time graphics applications, like video games or VR experiences, are among the most demanding workloads for any rendering API. These applications require high frame rates, low latency, and precise synchronization between the CPU and GPU. WebGPU, despite its promise of high performance, often falls short in these areas. The API's inherent overhead, combined with browser-related limitations, makes it difficult to achieve the smooth, responsive performance required for real-time applications. Frame drops, stuttering, and latency issues are common complaints from developers trying to use WebGPU for intensive graphics workloads.

8.5 The Multi-Threading Myth: Concurrency and Parallelism Issues

8.5.1 Thread Management Woes: Why WebGPU Fails to Exploit Multi-Core Systems

Modern GPUs and CPUs are designed to handle multiple tasks simultaneously through multi-threading and parallel processing.

However, WebGPU struggles to fully exploit these capabilities. Thread management in WebGPU is far from optimal, with developers frequently encountering issues related to race conditions, deadlocks, and poor synchronization. These problems prevent WebGPU from taking full advantage of multi-core systems, limiting its potential performance gains. Without efficient thread management, WebGPU's performance can be significantly hampered, especially in applications that rely heavily on parallel processing.

8.5.2 Synchronization Overhead: The Cost of Keeping Threads in Line

While multi-threading can boost performance by running multiple operations concurrently, it also introduces the need for synchronization between threads to ensure they don't conflict with each other. In WebGPU, this synchronization adds significant overhead, as the API must constantly manage the interactions between threads. This overhead can negate many of the potential performance gains from multi-threading, especially when running complex applications. As a result, developers often find that WebGPU's performance in multi-threaded environments is no better—if not worse—than single-threaded execution.

8.6 Summary

One of the core challenges in WebGPU's design is balancing parallelism with stability. While parallel processing can theoretically improve performance, it also increases the complexity of the system, making it more prone to errors and crashes. WebGPU's current implementation often sacrifices stability for speed, leading to unpredictable performance. In cases where parallelism is pushed too far, developers may encounter crashes or performance degradation, making WebGPU an unreliable option for high-performance applications. The trade-offs between parallelism and stability remain a significant barrier to WebGPU's performance ambitions.

9
Chapter

A Fragmented Future: Lack of Cross-Platform Support

Quote: "It's not a faith in technology. It's faith in people." (**Steve Jobs**)

9.1 Introduction

As of now, not all major platforms have embraced WebGPU. This includes some mobile operating systems, where the cost of implementation and performance concerns have caused hesitation. Similarly, some older desktop environments and certain browsers, especially those with niche user bases, have deprioritized WebGPU in favor of other API standards. The lack of WebGPU on these platforms leaves developers in a difficult position, having to either maintain WebGL compatibility or exclude segments of their audience. This absence also undermines WebGPU's claim of being a universal solution, as developers cannot rely on it to reach all users.

9.1.1 Adoption Disparities: Why the WebGPU Experience Differs Across Devices

Even on platforms that support WebGPU, the user experience can vary dramatically. High-end desktops might deliver seamless performance with WebGPU's capabilities, while lower-end devices—particularly older smartphones or tablets—struggle to meet the API's requirements. This disparity is compounded by the fact that manufacturers prioritize different aspects of WebGPU implementation, leading to inconsistent performance across devices. While desktop GPUs may offer strong support for parallel processing, mobile GPUs could suffer from memory constraints, causing applications to run slowly or crash altogether. These disparities diminish WebGPU's promise of a uniform web graphics experience.

9.2 Platform-Specific Feature Gaps

9.2.1 Feature Inconsistencies: What Works on One Platform But Not on Others

One of the most frustrating aspects of WebGPU's current consistency in its feature set across platforms. Some platforms may implement advanced features like compute shaders or support for high-end graphics, while others may lack these capabilities due to hardware or software limitations. For example, desktop environments with powerful GPUs may support more complex WebGPU features, while mobile platforms may not implement the same level of support, limiting developers who want to create cross-platform applications. This fragmentation makes it difficult for developers to know which features they can reliably use, forcing them to develop fallback solutions or alternative implementations that degrade the experience for users on less capable platforms.

9.2.2 The Browser Divide: Native vs. WebGPU Implementations

A key challenge WebGPU faces is the difference between native platform implementations and browser-based implementations. While WebGPU is designed to provide a high-performance, low-level API for web applications, browsers introduce overhead that native applications do not face. Browsers must prioritize security, sandboxing, and cross-platform compatibility, which can hinder performance and limit access to certain GPU features. Additionally, each browser has its own rendering engine, which can result in discrepancies in how WebGPU is implemented and executed. This can cause developers to encounter browser-specific bugs or performance bottlenecks, further fragmenting the development process.

9.2.3 Performance Differences: How WebGPU Varies Across Operating Systems

Operating system (OS) differences play a significant role in WebGPU's performance and functionality. Each OS interacts with hardware in unique ways, and the APIs they expose to developers can significantly impact WebGPU's efficiency. For example, WebGPU on Windows may rely on Direct3D, while macOS uses Metal, leading to inherent differences in how WebGPU operates. These underlying APIs have their own performance characteristics, optimizations, and limitations, which affect WebGPU's performance and feature set. Developers must account for these variations, further complicating cross-platform development efforts and leading to a non-uniform experience for end users.

Food for Thought - Innovative Technologies That Fell Short: **Palm Pilot** (Late 1990s–2000s) - The PDA Pioneer that Missed the Smartphone Revolution - Though hugely popular in its heyday, Palm's failure to transition effectively into the smartphone era caused it to fade into history, with later efforts like webOS coming too little, too late.

9.3 Driver Dependencies: A Hidden Problem

9.3.1 The Role of GPU Drivers: Why WebGPU Relies on Vendor Updates

GPU drivers serve as the bridge between WebGPU and the underlying hardware. However, WebGPU's reliance on these drivers introduces a major dependency that can lead to instability. Drivers are notoriously inconsistent across different vendors, and some hardware manufacturers are slower to release updates or patches. This creates a situation where WebGPU's functionality is dependent on driver support, and any issues with drivers—whether related to performance or security—can cause WebGPU to break or behave unpredictably. Moreover, drivers are often optimized for specific platforms or use cases, which can further fragment the WebGPU experience.

9.3.2 Driver Fragmentation: How Different Vendors Handle WebGPU Support

Different hardware vendors—NVIDIA, AMD, Intel, and others—handle WebGPU implementation in unique ways, leading to variability in how WebGPU performs on different systems. Each vendor has its own priorities, optimizations, and known issues, which can result in unpredictable behavior. For instance, a game or application that runs smoothly on an NVIDIA GPU may encounter performance issues or bugs when run on an AMD GPU due to differences in how each company handles shader compilation or memory management. These differences force developers to spend extra time testing and optimizing their code across various hardware setups, a burden that undermines WebGPU's promise of universality.

9.3.3 Stability Issues: When Driver Problems Cause Inconsistencies

Driver issues are a common source of instability when using WebGPU. A single buggy driver can crash an application or degrade performance significantly. For example, a new driver update from a GPU vendor might introduce changes that conflict with how WebGPU is supposed to function, resulting in instability that developers have little control over. These issues are compounded by the fact that users often run outdated drivers, creating a mismatch between the developer's testing environment and the user's system. In such cases, it's difficult to ensure a stable, consistent experience across all devices, making driver management a key challenge in WebGPU development.

9.4 Integration Challenges with Existing Tools and APIs

9.4.1 Middleware Mismatches: Why Current Tools Struggle with WebGPU

Many existing middleware solutions, such as game engines and graphic libraries, were built around older APIs like OpenGL, Direct3D, or Vulkan. Integrating WebGPU into these frameworks often leads to compatibility issues, as WebGPU's design and architecture differ significantly from these older APIs. For instance, engines like Unity or Unreal may not fully support WebGPU, forcing developers to work around missing features or incomplete integrations. This adds extra layers of complexity to the development process and increases the likelihood of bugs or performance issues, especially in larger projects that rely heavily on middleware.

9.4.2 Legacy System Integration: The High Cost of Bridging Old Technologies

One of the greatest challenges of adopting WebGPU is maintaining compatibility with older systems and technologies. Many applications, particularly in enterprise settings, still rely on legacy

APIs like WebGL. Transitioning to WebGPU means either abandoning support for these older systems or creating complex bridges between the two technologies, which can be resource-intensive and fraught with technical challenges. This often forces developers to choose between embracing the potential of WebGPU and maintaining broad compatibility with older, widely used systems, a trade-off that limits the API's immediate usefulness.

9.4.3 Development Workflow Disruptions: Fragmentation's Impact on Developer Efficiency

The fragmentation caused by WebGPU's inconsistent platform support and its differences from other APIs can significantly disrupt established development workflows. Developers accustomed to OpenGL or Direct3D may struggle with WebGPU's unique abstractions, leading to slower development cycles as teams adapt to the new API. Moreover, the need to test across multiple platforms with varying levels of WebGPU support introduces additional overhead. This creates bottlenecks in the production pipeline, increasing costs and reducing the efficiency of development teams—particularly in industries where time-to-market is crucial, like gaming and interactive media.

9.5 The Long-Term Outlook for Cross-Platform Consistency

9.5.1 The Push for Universal Standards: Can WebGPU Keep Up?

As WebGPU continues to evolve, there is a strong push within the industry to create more universal standards for cross-platform graphics. However, the current state of WebGPU reveals how far the industry still has to go. Competing APIs, platform-specific optimizations, and the slow adoption of new technologies mean that true cross-platform consistency is still a distant goal. While WebGPU aims to unify graphics programming across web and native platforms, its success depends on broader industry collaboration and a commitment from all major players to adopt and support it fully. Until then, fragmentation will remain a significant issue.

9.5.2 The API Race: Competing Standards That Threaten WebGPU's Future

WebGPU is not the only API vying for dominance in the graphics space. Other APIs like Vulkan, Metal, and Direct3D continue to evolve and offer their own solutions to cross-platform development. These APIs often have more mature ecosystems, better performance optimizations, and wider support from hardware manufacturers. As a result, many developers remain hesitant to fully commit to WebGPU, fearing that it may not achieve the industry-wide adoption needed to succeed. This competition could hinder WebGPU's growth, as developers are forced to weigh the benefits of WebGPU against the more established alternatives.

9.6 Summary

For WebGPU to truly be future-proof, it needs to address several critical issues, including performance, compatibility, and support across a wide range of devices. The growing complexity of hardware, the rise of new computing paradigms like quantum and AI acceleration, and the continued development of competing APIs all pose challenges to WebGPU's long-term viability. To remain relevant, WebGPU must evolve quickly and adapt to the changing technological landscape. Whether it can do so while overcoming its current fragmentation issues remains an open question, one that developers will watch closely as the API matures.

Chapter 10

The Learning Curve Trap: Is WebGPU Too Complex?

Quote: "Technological progress has merely provided us with more efficient means for going backwards." (**Aldous Huxley**)

10.1 Introduction

One of the most significant challenges of WebGPU is the need for developers to understand the underlying hardware. WebGPU is much closer to native APIs like Vulkan and Direct3D, which means that developers must now consider details like GPU pipelines, synchronization, and memory management. This requires a deeper knowledge of GPU architectures, something that was largely unnecessary with WebGL. For instance, a developer now needs to think about how memory is allocated across the GPU, how different threads are synchronized, and how shaders are optimized for the hardware. Without this knowledge, it is easy to make mistakes that can cripple performance or cause bugs that are difficult to debug.

10.1.1 More Control, More Complexity: The Cost of Power

WebGPU's promise of greater control over the GPU comes at the cost of increased complexity. For example, in WebGPU, developers need to manually manage shader pipelines and buffers, tasks that were previously handled automatically by WebGL. While this control is a powerful tool for optimizing performance, it also means that developers are now responsible for handling low-level operations that they may not be familiar with. This complexity can be overwhelming, particularly for smaller development teams or individual developers who may lack the resources to invest in mastering the intricacies of WebGPU. As a result, while WebGPU can theoretically produce more performant applications, the effort required to achieve this can be prohibitively high for many developers.

10.2 Steep Learning Curve for Newcomers

10.2.1 The Burden on Beginners: Why WebGPU Isn't for Everyone

For beginners entering the world of web-based graphics, WebGPU can be an intimidating first step. While WebGL offered a relatively gentle introduction to GPU programming, WebGPU demands a much higher level of technical skill right from the outset. Developers need to understand concepts such as memory layout, thread synchronization, and pipeline configuration to write even basic programs. This high entry barrier can discourage newcomers from using WebGPU, pushing them to either simpler APIs or entirely different platforms for graphics programming. The difficulty in grasping WebGPU's core concepts may prevent it from becoming the widely adopted standard it aims to be.

10.2.2 Lack of Learning Resources: Where Are the Tutorials?

One of the key issues with WebGPU is the lack of comprehensive learning resources. While the API is still relatively new, the absence of well-developed tutorials, books, and courses makes it even harder for developers to climb the learning curve. In contrast, WebGL has a wealth of learning materials, from beginner tutorials to advanced guides, which have helped foster a large community of developers. WebGPU, on the other hand, still suffers from a dearth of instructional content, leaving many developers to rely on sparse documentation or trial and error. Without a more robust ecosystem of learning resources, WebGPU's complexity will continue to act as a barrier to entry.

10.2.3 Stepping Stones: The Need for Intermediate Tools

To mitigate WebGPU's steep learning curve, there is a growing demand for intermediate tools or libraries that abstract some of the complexity without sacrificing the power that WebGPU offers. In the same way that libraries like Three.js simplified WebGL development, similar solutions are needed for WebGPU. These tools could provide higher-level abstractions that make it easier for developers to get started, while still allowing them to dig into WebGPU's low-level features as they become more comfortable. Without these stepping stones, WebGPU risks alienating a large segment of the development community who are eager to experiment with modern graphics but are put off by the API's steep learning curve.

Food for Thought - Innovative Technologies That Fell Short: **HD DVD** (2006) - The Format War Casualty - Locked in a bitter war with Blu-ray, HD DVD had early momentum but was ultimately outmaneuvered by Blu-ray, thanks in part to industry alliances and Sony's PlayStation 3 adopting the rival format.

10.3 The Challenges of Modern Graphics Development

10.3.1 Modern Graphics Programming: Not for the Faint of Heart

Developing modern, high-performance graphics applications is already a complex task, even with well-established APIs like OpenGL or DirectX. WebGPU further amplifies this complexity by introducing an API that operates at a lower level, requiring developers to handle aspects of GPU management that are often abstracted away in other APIs. For example, WebGPU demands a deep understanding of shader programming and memory optimization to achieve high-performance rendering. While this level of control can lead to significant performance gains, it also increases the risk of introducing bugs or inefficiencies that can be difficult to track down and fix. This complexity raises the question of whether WebGPU's design is truly suited for the average developer.

10.3.2 The Performance Trap: Why Complexity Doesn't Always Lead to Speed

Despite WebGPU's potential for greater performance, its complexity can sometimes negate the benefits it promises. Without careful optimization, developers can easily write inefficient WebGPU code that performs worse than simpler WebGL applications. For instance, failing to manage GPU resources properly or creating in-efficient shader programs can lead to bottlenecks that slow down rendering times. This performance trap is particularly dangerous for developers who are still learning the intricacies of the API, as they may assume that using WebGPU automatically guarantees better performance, only to find that their applications run slower than expected.

10.4 Real-World Development Concerns

10.4.1 Team Training: The Investment Required to Master We-bGPU

For teams adopting WebGPU, a significant investment in training and education is often required. Even experienced developers who are familiar with older APIs like WebGL or DirectX will need time to get up to speed with WebGPU's unique design. This means that companies looking to take advantage of WebGPU's capabilities will need to allocate time and resources to ensure that their teams can effectively use the new API. For smaller teams or companies operating on tight deadlines, this training requirement may be a major deterrent to adopting WebGPU, especially when other APIs or technologies might offer similar results with less upfront effort.

10.4.2 Debugging Challenges: The Complexity of Troubleshoot-ing

One of the most frustrating aspects of working with WebGPU is the difficulty of debugging. Because WebGPU operates at such a low level, errors in memory management, synchronization, or pipeline configuration can lead to crashes or unexpected behav-ior that is difficult to trace. Unlike higher-level APIs, where de-bugging tools and error messages can offer meaningful guidance, WebGPU's error reporting is often cryptic or nonexistent. This lack of robust debugging tools further complicates the learning process, as developers are left to manually sift through their code to identify and resolve issues.

10.5 Summary

The complexity of WebGPU presents a significant challenge for developers. While the API offers unprecedented control over GPU resources and the potential for improved performance, the learn-ing curve may be too steep for many developers to justify the transition. Without more accessible learning resources, better debugging tools, and intermediate libraries to bridge the gap between WebGL and WebGPU, the API risks alienating both newcomers and seasoned developers alike. The question remains: is WebGPU's complexity an inevitable consequence of its power, or could the API be designed in a way that offers both flexibility and accessibility? Until these issues are addressed, WebGPU may remain an advanced tool for a select group of developers, rather than the broadly adopted standard it aims to become.

11
Chapter

Debugging Hell: How WebGPU Makes Troubleshooting Harder

Quote: "The only way to discover the limits of the possible is to go beyond them into the impossible." (**Arthur C. Clarke**)

11.1 Introduction

One of the core reasons why WebGPU is so difficult to debug is its level of abstraction. Although it abstracts away some of the complexities found in native APIs like Vulkan, it still operates much closer to the hardware than older standards like WebGL. This reduced layer of abstraction means that developers are responsible for managing tasks such as memory allocation, buffer synchronization, and shader pipelines—any mistakes in these areas can have disastrous consequences. For example, if a developer fails to synchronize threads properly or mismanages GPU memory, the result can be performance degradation, graphical glitches, or even system crashes. Because these errors occur at such a low level, they are often difficult to diagnose without specialized tools.

11.1.1 Real-World Example: Debugging Synchronization Failures

Consider a real-world example of debugging a synchronization failure in WebGPU. If a developer inadvertently causes two threads to access the same GPU memory simultaneously without proper locking or synchronization, the results can be unpredictable. The program might work fine during testing, but crash intermittently under higher loads. The challenge lies in identifying where the synchronization issue occurs, as WebGPU does not provide detailed error messages or stack traces for these kinds of low-level issues. Developers are left to manually inspect their code, adding logging statements or trying to reproduce the issue in different environments to track down the elusive bug. This process can be time-consuming and frustrating, especially for those who lack experience with low-level concurrency issues.

11.2 Limited Debugging Tools for WebGPU

One of the most significant hurdles for developers working with WebGPU is the lack of mature debugging tools. Unlike more established graphics APIs like DirectX or OpenGL, which have had years to build up a robust ecosystem of debugging and profiling tools, WebGPU is still in its infancy. Tools that can visualize GPU workloads, trace memory usage, or provide insights into performance bottlenecks are either non-existent or highly experimental for WebGPU. This forces developers to rely on more manual methods of debugging, such as reviewing code line by line or using lower-level system profilers that may not fully support WebGPU's unique architecture.

11.2.1 The Absence of Breakpoints and Step-by-Step Debugging

A key feature that developers miss when debugging WebGPU applications is the ability to set breakpoints and step through their code in a meaningful way. In higher-level programming environments, breakpoints allow developers to pause the execution of a program and inspect variables or the state of the application at specific points. However, when working with WebGPU, especially in the browser, breakpoints offer limited utility because so much of the GPU workload happens outside the normal JavaScript execution environment. As a result, developers are left to infer the state of GPU operations indirectly, often by using logging or profiling techniques that provide incomplete information.

11.2.2 Debugging Shaders: The Invisible Code

Shaders, which are an essential component of any WebGPU application, present another set of debugging challenges. Shaders are typically written in a specialized language like WGSL (WebGPU

Shading Language) and executed directly on the GPU. When a shader fails, it often does so silently, without producing useful error messages or logs. Debugging shader code requires a deep understanding of both the GPU pipeline and the specific behavior of shaders on different hardware platforms. The process of identifying a faulty shader can be incredibly frustrating, as developers often have to modify code in small increments and rerun their application to isolate the problem. This trial-and-error approach makes shader debugging one of the most time-consuming aspects of WebGPU development.

Food for Thought - Innovative Technologies That Fell Short: **LaserDisc** (1978) - The Future of Home Video That Wasn't - LaserDisc offered better picture and sound quality than VHS but was expensive and inconvenient due to the large, fragile discs. It never gained mainstream adoption, although it found a niche among film enthusiasts.

11.3 The Difficulty of Reproducing Bugs

Bugs that occur in WebGPU are often difficult to reproduce consistently, adding another layer of frustration for developers. Many issues arise from concurrency problems, race conditions, or hardware-specific behavior, all of which can vary depending on the environment in which the application is running. A bug that only occurs on a specific GPU or under a certain workload might be impossible to reproduce on a developer's machine, making it harder to identify the root cause. This inconsistency leads to situations where bugs are reported by users but cannot be easily reproduced by the development team, delaying fixes and frustrating both developers and users alike.

11.3.1 Concurrency and Race Conditions: Elusive Bugs That Appear Only Under Load

Concurrency issues, such as race conditions, are particularly challenging to reproduce because they depend on the timing of operations in a multi-threaded environment. These bugs might only manifest under specific conditions, such as when the system is under heavy load or when multiple applications are competing for GPU resources. For instance, a developer might build an application that works perfectly during testing, only to have it fail intermittently in production. The root cause could be a race condition where two threads access the same memory simultaneously, but tracking down this issue can be like finding a needle in a haystack due to the unpredictable nature of concurrent execution. Without the proper debugging tools, developers are forced to make educated guesses and rely on extensive testing to find and fix these issues.

11.4 Cryptic Error Messages and Lack of Documentation

One of the most common complaints from developers working with WebGPU is the cryptic or nonexistent error messages they encounter when things go wrong. Error messages that fail to provide actionable information slow down the debugging process and leave developers in the dark about the underlying issue. Often, WebGPU will simply fail silently, with no indication of what caused the problem. Even when error messages are provided, they tend to be vague or overly technical, requiring developers to dig into GPU documentation or source code to understand what went wrong. This lack of clear communication between the API and the developer is a major roadblock to efficient debugging.

11.4.1 The Documentation Gap: How Poor Documentation Compounds Debugging Challenges

Compounding these issues is the fact that WebGPU's documentation is still incomplete in many areas. While WebGPU is actively evolving, the rapid pace of development means that official documentation often lags behind the current state of the API. This creates gaps in the information available to developers, leaving them to experiment with different approaches or search through online forums for solutions. For example, a developer might encounter an error related to memory management but find that the documentation does not fully explain how WebGPU handles memory allocation and deallocation. This forces developers to rely on trial and error, further complicating an already difficult debugging process.

11.5 Debugging in the Browser: A Layer of Complexity

WebGPU's integration into the web environment adds another layer of complexity to the debugging process. Unlike native APIs, which can be debugged using tools designed specifically for desktop applications, WebGPU runs inside the browser, where additional layers of abstraction obscure the underlying operations. The interaction between WebGPU, JavaScript, and the browser's rendering engine can lead to performance bottlenecks and errors that are difficult to diagnose. For instance, developers may encounter issues that arise not from their WebGPU code but from how the browser handles GPU resources or schedules rendering tasks. These browser-specific quirks make debugging even more difficult, as developers must contend with both the browser environment and WebGPU's low-level intricacies.

11.5.1 JavaScript Debugging vs. GPU Debugging: Different Worlds

The differences between JavaScript debugging and GPU debugging can be stark. In traditional JavaScript development, debugging tools are well-established and provide clear insights into variable states, function calls, and execution flow. However, when dealing with WebGPU, much of the work happens in the background on the GPU, outside the scope of typical JavaScript debugging tools. A developer may set breakpoints or analyze logs in their JavaScript code, only to find that the real issue lies deep within the GPU's execution pipeline. This disconnect between the JavaScript layer and the GPU layer forces developers to switch between different mental models, making the debugging process more complex and less intuitive.

11.6 Summary

The challenges of debugging WebGPU are numerous and significant, posing a substantial barrier to developers looking to leverage the full power of the API. The lack of mature debugging tools, cryptic error messages, and the inherent complexity of low-level GPU programming all contribute to a frustrating development experience. For WebGPU to reach its full potential, there is an urgent need for better debugging tools, clearer documentation, and more robust error reporting mechanisms. Until these issues are addressed, WebGPU will remain a powerful but difficult-to-use API, accessible only to those with the time, patience, and expertise to navigate its many debugging pitfalls.

12
Chapter

Unrealistic Promises: What WebGPU Said It Would Do

Quote: "Failure is simply the opportunity to begin again, this time more intelligently." (**Henry Ford**)

12.1 Introduction

One of the key selling points of WebGPU was the idea of platform independence. Developers were excited about the possibility of creating graphics applications that could run seamlessly on any operating system or browser, without needing to worry about specific platform requirements or hardware capabilities. Yet, this promise has not fully materialized. WebGPU's performance varies significantly depending on the platform, with some operating systems offering far better support than others. For instance, WebGPU performs well on modern Windows and macOS systems but faces challenges on Linux, mobile platforms, and older hardware. This fragmentation undermines the core promise of WebGPU, forcing developers to implement platform-specific optimizations and workarounds, contradicting the initial vision of simplicity and uniformity.

Another major promise of WebGPU was its supposed cross-browser compatibility. In theory, developers should be able to write WebGPU code once and have it run consistently in any browser that supports the API. However, in practice, different browsers have adopted WebGPU at varying paces, and the implementation quality differs. While Chrome and Firefox offer relatively robust support, other browsers like Safari have been slower to integrate WebGPU, leading to discrepancies in performance and functionality. This uneven adoption complicates the development process, as developers need to account for browser-specific quirks and inconsistencies, which was not part of the original promise.

12.2 Underestimating the Complexity of Low-Level Graphics Programming

WebGPU was marketed as an accessible API that would allow web developers to tap into the power of modern GPUs without needing the expertise required for lower-level APIs like Vulkan or DirectX. However, the reality has been that WebGPU is far more complex than initially expected. While it does abstract away some of the more arcane aspects of GPU programming, it still requires a solid understanding of parallelism, memory management, and graphics pipelines. Many developers, particularly those coming from a background in simpler web technologies, find WebGPU's low-level nature overwhelming. The steep learning curve has led to frustration and slower adoption, contradicting the promise that WebGPU would be easy to pick up for developers familiar with WebGL or higher-level APIs.

12.2.1 Ease of Use: The Illusion of Simplicity

The promise of WebGPU as an "easy-to-use" API was one of its most appealing features. Early announcements suggested that WebGPU would provide an accessible gateway to high-performance graphics programming for web developers, many of whom are not familiar with low-level GPU management. However, this promise has proven illusory. In reality, WebGPU requires deep knowledge of graphics programming concepts that are far removed from the typical skill set of a web developer. Tasks like managing memory buffers, writing shaders in WGSL, and ensuring correct synchronization between CPU and GPU operations introduce a level of complexity that most web developers are unprepared for. This gap between promise and reality has led to frustration, as many developers find themselves out of their depth when trying to implement advanced graphics features with WebGPU.

12.2.2 The Documentation Gap: Unsupported Claims of Simplicity

Part of the promise of WebGPU's ease of use was also tied to expectations of strong, detailed documentation that would guide developers through the intricacies of the API. Unfortunately, WebGPU's documentation has often been incomplete, inconsistent, or difficult to follow, leaving developers with little guidance as they navigate the complexities of the API. While some third-party resources have begun to fill the gap, the lack of official, comprehensive documentation has exacerbated the learning curve. This failure to provide sufficient educational materials has further eroded the promise of WebGPU being accessible to a broad range of developers, as many struggle to find reliable information on how to implement even basic features.

Food for Thought - Innovative Technologies That Fell Short: **MySpace** (2003) - The Social Network Pioneer That Fell to Facebook - MySpace was once the dominant social networking platform but lost its crown to Facebook due to poor management, a cluttered user interface, and the inability to adapt to changing user expectations.

12.3 Unmet Expectations for Performance Improvements

WebGPU was heavily promoted as a major performance upgrade over its predecessor, WebGL. The promise was that WebGPU would unlock the full power of modern GPUs for web applications, allowing for AAA-quality graphics and real-time performance. While WebGPU has undoubtedly provided performance improvements in certain scenarios, particularly for more complex applications, these gains have not been as universal or dramatic as initially promised. Many developers have reported that the performance improvements over WebGL are marginal at best, especially for simpler applications. In some cases, the overhead introduced by WebGPU's complexity has actually led to performance regressions, particularly on lower-end devices.

12.3.1 Graphics Fidelity: Overpromising on Visual Quality

One of the most exciting promises surrounding WebGPU was the ability to bring console-quality graphics to the web. In theory, WebGPU's low-level access to the GPU would allow developers to create web-based applications that could rival the graphical fidelity of native games or desktop applications. While WebGPU does provide more control over shaders, buffers, and pipelines, the promise of achieving native-like graphical quality on the web has not fully materialized. Limitations related to browser performance, hardware variability, and the complexity of writing efficient WebGPU code have all contributed to a gap between the promised graphical fidelity and what has been delivered in practice. Many developers find themselves still constrained by the limitations of web-based environments, even when using WebGPU.

12.3.2 Latency and Overhead: Performance Costs of a New API

Another area where WebGPU has struggled to meet its performance promises is latency. Although WebGPU provides developers with low-level control over GPU tasks, this often comes at the cost of increased complexity and overhead. Developers have to carefully manage synchronization between the CPU and GPU to avoid bottlenecks, and even small mistakes in resource management can lead to significant performance penalties. Furthermore, the fact that WebGPU operates within the browser environment adds an additional layer of overhead that native APIs do not face. These factors have led to disappointing performance in many cases, with developers finding that WebGPU doesn't always live up to its potential, especially in comparison to native graphics APIs like Vulkan or Metal.

12.4 The Misleading Promise of Universal Adoption

WebGPU's early marketing positioned it as the future of web-based graphics, suggesting that it would soon become the standard for rendering high-performance graphics in browsers. This promise created expectations that WebGPU would quickly be adopted across all major browsers and platforms, enabling developers to target a wide audience with a single API. However, the reality has been much slower adoption and more fragmented support than anticipated. While WebGPU has been implemented in some browsers, many platforms still lack full support. This fragmentation has created significant challenges for developers who were expecting a more unified environment. The promise of universal adoption remains far off, with many platforms either lagging behind or not supporting WebGPU at all.

12.4.1 The Struggle for Browser Support

One of the key factors that has hampered WebGPU's adoption is the uneven pace at which different browsers have implemented the API. While Google's Chrome and Mozilla's Firefox have been quick to embrace WebGPU, other browsers, particularly Apple's Safari, have been much slower to adopt the standard. This lack of consistent support across all major browsers has undermined the initial promise of WebGPU as a truly cross-platform API. Developers who were hoping to use WebGPU to create applications that work seamlessly across all platforms are instead faced with the reality of needing to implement fallback solutions for browsers that don't yet support the API.

12.5 Summary

WebGPU's promise of universal adoption has also been hampered by its incomplete support for mobile devices. While WebGPU performs well on modern desktop systems, its performance on mobile platforms has been inconsistent, with many devices lacking full support for the API. This has created a significant roadblock for developers who were hoping to bring high-performance graphics applications to mobile users. The promise of WebGPU as a cross-platform solution for both desktop and mobile has thus far fallen short, with many mobile devices either lacking the necessary hardware capabilities or not supporting the API at all.

13
Chapter

The Security Fixes No One Is Talking About

Quote: "Any sufficiently advanced technology is indistinguishable from magic." (**Arthur C. Clarke**)

13.1 Introduction

One of the most pressing issues surrounding WebGPU is the security vulnerabilities that have not been adequately addressed. While much of the conversation around WebGPU has focused on its performance and cross-platform capabilities, relatively little attention has been paid to the security risks it introduces. Unlike other APIs that have undergone years of rigorous testing and patching, WebGPU is still in its infancy, and many potential security flaws have yet to be fully explored or resolved. The combination of direct access to hardware resources and its low-level nature makes WebGPU particularly vulnerable to new forms of attacks, yet the security discussions remain limited.

WebGPU opens up significant attack vectors that haven't been widely discussed. With its direct access to the GPU, WebGPU can potentially expose the system to hardware-level attacks. This is especially concerning when considering the complexity of GPUs and the lack of visibility that developers and even security experts have into how these devices manage tasks. Attacks such as side-channel exploits, which were once relegated to CPU vulnerabilities, are now a threat for GPUs as well. The potential for malicious actors to exploit these weaknesses in browsers, particularly where sandboxing mechanisms may fall short, has created a silent threat that the industry isn't adequately addressing.

13.1.1 Inadequate Security Audits: A Gap in WebGPU's Development Cycle

While security audits are a standard part of the development process for mature APIs, WebGPU has not undergone the same level of scrutiny. The rush to develop WebGPU as a high-performance API for the web has meant that security concerns have often taken a backseat to performance optimizations and cross-platform functionality. As a result, many vulnerabilities remain unexamined or undiscovered. With so few thorough security audits conducted on WebGPU thus far, it's likely that critical flaws could be found in the future—flaws that may expose end-users to risks that haven't been fully accounted for by developers or the companies driving WebGPU's implementation.

Food for Thought - Innovative Technologies That Fell Short: **Pebble Smartwatch** (2013) - The Crowdfunding Darling That Couldn't Compete - Pebble was one of the first smartwatches and a crowdfunding success story, but despite its early lead, it couldn't keep pace with competitors like the Apple Watch and Android Wear devices, leading to its eventual shutdown.

13.2 The Need for GPU-Level Security Measures

WebGPU's design relies on giving web applications more direct access to the GPU than previous web APIs, such as WebGL. This access, while beneficial for performance, also introduces a host of security challenges. Traditionally, the operating system and browser have served as gatekeepers, limiting the damage that could be caused by malicious code. However, with WebGPU, developers are now able to write low-level shaders and manipulate GPU memory directly, which could lead to vulnerabilities that allow malicious actors to bypass traditional security mechanisms. Strengthening GPU-level security is critical, yet it remains a topic that hasn't been adequately discussed in the broader WebGPU discourse.

13.2.1 Memory Management: The Unseen Security Risk

One of the most significant risks introduced by WebGPU is related to memory management. With WebGPU, developers have the ability to allocate and manage GPU memory more directly, which opens up the possibility of memory leaks and buffer overflows. These types of issues can lead to severe security vulnerabilities, such as allowing an attacker to execute arbitrary code or cause a denial-of-service attack. Unlike CPUs, where memory management has long been a focus of security measures, GPUs are not as well understood or protected. This lack of focus on GPU memory vulnerabilities in WebGPU could open the door to exploits that many developers aren't prepared to defend against.

13.2.2 Race Conditions and Concurrency Issues: A New Class of Vulnerabilities

WebGPU's emphasis on parallelism and multi-threaded operations introduces another layer of complexity and security risk. Race conditions, where the timing of threads leads to unpredictable behavior, can create opportunities for malicious actors to interfere with a program's execution in unexpected ways. In WebGPU, where managing the GPU's concurrency is key to maximizing performance, these race conditions can lead to vulnerabilities that are difficult to detect or prevent. Existing solutions to address concurrency issues, like using locks or other synchronization mechanisms, are often inadequate in a WebGPU context because of the increased complexity and speed at which the GPU operates.

13.3 The Role of Browser Vendors in Security

Much of WebGPU's security ultimately depends on how well browser vendors implement the API. Each browser is responsible for integrating WebGPU in a way that maximizes security without sacrificing too much performance. This delicate balancing act has proven to be challenging, as vendors are often caught between ensuring that WebGPU runs smoothly and protecting the user from potential security risks. Some browsers have implemented more stringent sandboxing measures than others, but there are still gaps in how browsers approach WebGPU's security. In the rush to keep up with performance and feature demands, many vendors have not prioritized the security fixes that are necessary to protect users.

13.3.1 Browser Sandboxing: A Weak Shield Against WebGPU Attacks

Sandboxing has traditionally been one of the key mechanisms that browsers use to isolate web applications from the underlying system. However, WebGPU's low-level access to the GPU threatens to undermine the effectiveness of these sandboxes. Because WebGPU operates closer to the hardware than previous APIs, the risk of a successful sandbox escape is higher. While browser vendors have implemented some protective measures, such as limiting certain high-risk operations or requiring user permissions, these mitigations are often incomplete. For instance, side-channel attacks that exploit GPU timing information can still bypass many of these defenses, and it's unclear whether existing sandboxing techniques are sufficient to address these new threats.

13.3.2 Vendor-Specific Patches: Inconsistent Security Measures Across Browsers

One of the key challenges with WebGPU security is that browser vendors are implementing their own patches and security fixes independently. This has led to a fragmented security landscape, where some browsers are more secure than others. For example, Chrome may implement fixes for certain GPU vulnerabilities faster than Firefox, or Safari may have different priorities when it comes to addressing memory management issues. This inconsistency makes it difficult for developers to rely on WebGPU as a secure API, since the security measures vary from browser to browser. Without a coordinated effort among vendors, these security discrepancies will continue to undermine the broader WebGPU ecosystem.

13.4 Security Best Practices: What Developers Should Be Doing

Developers have a crucial role to play in ensuring that WebGPU applications are secure. However, many developers are not well-versed in the security implications of using a low-level graphics API like WebGPU. In fact, security best practices for WebGPU development are not widely discussed or documented, leaving developers without clear guidance on how to avoid common pitfalls. The lack of educational resources and tools to help developers write secure WebGPU code is one of the most glaring gaps in the ecosystem. To prevent the next major security incident, developers need better access to tools, documentation, and frameworks that prioritize security from the outset.

13.4.1 Auditing WebGPU Code: A Crucial, Yet Overlooked Practice

One of the most important steps developers can take to ensure security in WebGPU applications is performing regular code audits. Because WebGPU allows for low-level access to hardware, even small mistakes in the code can lead to significant vulnerabilities. Auditing WebGPU code for memory leaks, buffer overflows, and race conditions is essential, but it's a practice that many developers are unfamiliar with. Furthermore, the tools that exist for auditing WebGPU code are still in their infancy, making it difficult for even experienced developers to identify and fix potential security issues. Without widespread adoption of auditing practices, WebGPU will continue to be a high-risk platform for security vulnerabilities.

13.4.2 Security Testing Frameworks: The Missing Link in WebGPU Development

Another critical tool that is currently lacking in the WebGPU ecosystem is a comprehensive security testing framework. While testing frameworks exist for performance benchmarking and functionality testing, there are few robust solutions for security testing in WebGPU applications. Developers need tools that can automatically detect common vulnerabilities like memory mismanagement, race conditions, and sandbox escapes. Without such tools, developers are left to manually inspect their code for security issues, a process that is both time-consuming and error-prone. The development of a strong security testing framework is essential if WebGPU is to achieve the level of security that modern web applications demand.

13.5 Summary

As WebGPU continues to evolve, the need for a stronger focus on security will only become more critical. While the API has made impressive strides in terms of performance and functionality, its security measures are still lagging behind. To ensure that WebGPU becomes a viable option for high-performance web applications, the community must take a more proactive approach to identifying and addressing security risks. This includes coordinated efforts between browser vendors, GPU manufacturers, and developers to create a more secure ecosystem for WebGPU.

The question remains: can WebGPU be secured in the long term? The answer depends on how quickly the community can develop and implement the necessary security measures. This will require a shift in focus from performance optimization to security prioritization. Browser vendors must take the lead in implementing more stringent sandboxing techniques and ensuring that WebGPU's vulnerabilities are addressed as soon as they are discovered. Meanwhile, developers must adopt security best practices and push for the creation of better tools and frameworks for auditing and testing WebGPU code. If these steps are taken, WebGPU could become a secure and reliable API, but without them, it will remain a high-risk platform.

One of the key factors in securing WebGPU will be the standardization of security practices across browsers and platforms. Currently, the fragmented nature of WebGPU's development means that security measures are inconsistent, which only exacerbates its vulnerabilities. A standardized approach to security, where all major browsers and platforms adhere to the same guidelines and best practices, is essential for reducing the risk of exploitation. This could involve creating a set of security standards for WebGPU, similar to what exists for other web technologies like HTTPS or CSP (Content Security Policy). With a standardized security framework in place, WebGPU can become the powerful, secure API that was originally promised.

14
Chapter

GPU Access, but at What Cost?

Quote: "If you want to make an apple pie from scratch, you must first create the universe." (**Carl Sagan**)

Quote: "Every once in a while, a new technology, an old problem, and a big idea turn into an innovation." (**Dean Kamen**)

14.1 Introduction

The performance improvements enabled by WebGPU can come at the cost of user safety and system integrity. The ability to push the GPU harder than before may lead to unintended consequences, such as increased power consumption, overheating, or even hardware damage in extreme cases. Additionally, if developers prioritize performance over stability, they may inadvertently create applications that crash or behave unpredictably under certain conditions. This unchecked pursuit of performance, without adequate safeguards in place, creates an environment where users may experience issues like system instability or data loss, all in the name of higher frame rates or faster rendering.

While WebGPU does provide the opportunity for immense performance gains, ensuring that those gains do not compromise security or stability requires additional safeguards, many of which introduce overhead. Error handling, resource management, and security checks all consume processing power that could otherwise be directed toward improving performance. As a result, developers face a dilemma: implement the necessary protections and risk losing the performance edge, or bypass these checks in favor of speed, potentially putting users at risk. This delicate balance between maintaining performance and implementing safeguards is one of the major challenges that WebGPU presents to developers.

14.2 Power Consumption and Efficiency Concerns

WebGPU's direct access to the GPU not only raises security issues but also presents challenges in terms of power consumption and efficiency. While developers can take advantage of the GPU's processing power to achieve better graphical performance, they must also be mindful of the energy costs associated with these improvements. Power-hungry applications can drain battery life on mobile devices and cause systems to throttle performance to manage heat. These factors can significantly reduce the actual benefits of WebGPU, especially in contexts where energy efficiency is critical, such as mobile gaming or VR applications.

14.2.1 Battery Drain: The Cost of Pushing the GPU

One of the major concerns with giving developers more control over the GPU is the potential for excessive power consumption. On mobile devices, where battery life is a primary concern, applications that heavily utilize the GPU can quickly drain the battery, leading to a poor user experience. Even in desktop environments, excessive GPU usage can lead to higher energy bills and an increased carbon footprint, as the hardware is pushed to its limits for prolonged periods. These hidden costs of GPU access often go unnoticed, but they can have a significant impact on both users and the environment.

14.2.2 Thermal Throttling: When Performance Hits a Wall

As WebGPU enables developers to fully utilize the GPU, it also increases the likelihood of running into thermal throttling issues. When the GPU overheats due to excessive load, the system may automatically reduce performance to prevent hardware damage. This throttling can lead to a significant decrease in performance, negating the benefits of WebGPU's direct access. For users, this means that while an application may initially run smoothly, prolonged use or high-intensity workloads could cause the system to slow down dramatically. In many cases, developers may not account for thermal management in their designs, leading to inconsistent performance across different devices.

Food for Thought - Innovative Technologies That Fell Short: **3D TV** (2010s) - The Gimmick That Never Caught On - 3D TVs were heavily marketed as the next big thing in home entertainment, but high costs, a lack of compelling 3D content, and the inconvenience of wearing 3D glasses led to consumer disinterest and the technology's quick fade from the market.

14.3 The Complexity of Resource Management

With WebGPU's low-level access comes the added complexity of resource management. Developers are now responsible for managing GPU memory, synchronizing tasks, and optimizing workloads to ensure efficient performance. However, this complexity often leads to issues such as memory leaks, resource contention, and inefficient use of hardware resources. The cost of managing these resources effectively can slow down development times and introduce new bugs, making WebGPU more challenging to work with than higher-level APIs. Additionally, mismanagement of these resources can lead to performance degradation, even on high-end systems, as the GPU is not used to its full potential.

14.3.1 Memory Leaks and Resource Exhaustion

One of the most common problems in WebGPU development is managing GPU memory efficiently. Unlike higher-level APIs that abstract away many of the details of memory management, WebGPU places the responsibility squarely on the developer's shoulders. This can lead to issues such as memory leaks, where the application fails to release memory after it is no longer needed. Over time, these leaks can cause the system to slow down or even crash as it runs out of available memory. Resource exhaustion is particularly problematic in long-running applications, such as games or interactive experiences, where memory management must be precise to avoid performance degradation.

14.3.2 Synchronization and Task Management Woes

Another significant challenge of WebGPU is ensuring that tasks are properly synchronized across multiple threads or processes. GPU programming often involves parallel execution of tasks, but without proper synchronization, tasks can interfere with each other, leading to unpredictable results or performance bottlenecks. For developers, this adds another layer of complexity to an already difficult problem. Poor synchronization can lead to race conditions, where the order in which tasks are executed affects the outcome, potentially causing errors or crashes. Managing this complexity effectively requires deep knowledge of concurrent programming, which many developers may lack when transitioning to WebGPU.

14.4 Hidden Maintenance Costs: The Burden on Developers

While WebGPU promises high performance and direct hardware access, it also places a significant burden on developers to maintain and optimize their code. Unlike higher-level APIs that abstract away many of the complexities of GPU programming, WebGPU requires developers to take full responsibility for managing resources, optimizing performance, and ensuring stability. This added responsibility increases development time and makes maintenance more difficult, as even small changes to the codebase can introduce new bugs or performance issues. The cost of maintaining a WebGPU-based project is higher than many developers anticipate, particularly when considering the need for ongoing optimization and debugging.

14.4.1 Debugging Challenges: Finding the Source of Performance Problems

One of the most frustrating aspects of working with WebGPU is the difficulty in identifying and resolving performance problems. Because WebGPU operates at such a low level, issues like memory leaks, synchronization errors, and inefficient resource usage can be difficult to track down. Many of the traditional debugging tools used for higher-level APIs are inadequate for WebGPU, requiring developers to rely on more specialized tools that may not be as well-documented or widely available. This makes the debugging process slower and more error-prone, further increasing the cost of developing and maintaining WebGPU applications.

14.5 Summary

Optimizing WebGPU applications for performance is not a one-time task; it requires ongoing effort throughout the development lifecycle. As hardware evolves, new optimization opportunities may arise, but taking advantage of them often requires significant changes to the codebase. Additionally, optimizations that work well on one device may not translate to other platforms, necessitating platform-specific tweaks to ensure consistent performance. This constant need for optimization can be a drain on development resources, particularly for small teams or independent developers who may not have the time or expertise to continually fine-tune their applications for maximum performance.

15
Chapter

WebGPU vs. WebGL: Is Progress Really Progress?

Quote: "Many of life's failures are people who did not realize how close they were to success when they gave up." (**Thomas Edison**)

15.1 Introduction

WebGL, introduced in 2011, revolutionized web graphics by bringing hardware-accelerated 3D rendering to web browsers using the GPU. It allowed developers to create complex 3D graphics in web applications without requiring users to install additional plugins. WebGL built on OpenGL ES, which had already seen success in mobile and embedded systems, ensuring that it had a stable, proven foundation. In contrast, WebGPU represents a more modern approach, designed to give developers more direct control over the GPU, offering performance gains and greater flexibility. However, while WebGPU aims to replace WebGL, the transition has not been as smooth as many hoped.

One of WebGL's biggest strengths is its stability and wide adoption across platforms and browsers. Over the years, it has been thoroughly tested, refined, and supported by the vast majority of web browsers, making it a reliable choice for developers looking to incorporate 3D graphics into their web applications. Its underlying architecture, based on OpenGL ES, has ensured that WebGL enjoys a long history of cross-platform compatibility. As a result, WebGL has been embraced by developers and content creators alike, with countless applications, games, and tools leveraging its capabilities. WebGPU, while promising, has yet to match this level of adoption and stability, leading many to question whether it truly represents progress.

15.1.1 WebGPU's Ambition: More Power, More Complexity

WebGPU's primary goal is to offer more direct control over the GPU, providing developers with the ability to create higher-performance applications. It introduces features that were not possible with WebGL, such as compute shaders and more fine-grained memory management. This increased power allows developers to push the limits of what can be achieved in the browser, particularly for graphics-heavy applications such as games, virtual reality (VR), and complex data visualizations. However, with this increased power comes increased complexity. WebGPU's API is lower-level and requires a more detailed understanding of GPU architecture, making it harder for developers to pick up and use effectively compared to the more abstracted WebGL.

15.2 Performance vs. Usability: Is WebGPU Worth the Effort?

While WebGPU promises better performance than WebGL, the question remains whether this performance improvement is worth the added complexity and effort required from developers. WebGL's simplicity and wide adoption have made it an easy choice for many developers, even those with limited experience in GPU programming. In contrast, WebGPU demands a much deeper understanding of both the hardware and the API itself. The learning curve for WebGPU is significantly steeper, and for many use cases, the performance gains may not be substantial enough to justify the additional effort.

15.2.1 Performance Gains: How Much Faster Is WebGPU?

In theory, WebGPU should outperform WebGL in nearly every scenario, given its closer access to the GPU and more modern design. Benchmarks in controlled environments have shown that WebGPU can offer significant performance improvements, especially in compute-heavy applications or those that require advanced rendering techniques. However, these performance gains are often difficult to realize in real-world applications due to the added complexity of managing GPU resources, synchronization, and memory allocation. For simpler use cases, where WebGL already performs adequately, the gains offered by WebGPU may not be significant enough to warrant the switch. This leaves developers questioning whether WebGPU's added complexity is justified by the potential performance improvements.

15.2.2 Developer Usability: A Steep Learning Curve

The usability gap between WebGL and WebGPU is perhaps the most significant barrier to adoption. WebGL's API, while based on the older OpenGL ES, is well-documented and relatively easy to learn for developers familiar with 3D graphics programming. WebGPU, on the other hand, introduces a much more complex and lower-level API, requiring developers to handle tasks such as memory management and synchronization that WebGL abstracts away. This additional complexity makes WebGPU more difficult to use effectively, especially for developers who are not experienced with modern GPU programming. As a result, many developers may find WebGPU too challenging to work with, particularly for smaller projects where the performance benefits may not justify the additional effort.

Food for Thought - Innovative Technologies That Fell Short: **Amazon Fire Phone** (2014) - A Smartphone Misfire - Amazon's Fire Phone was an ambitious attempt to enter the smartphone market. However, its high price, lack of distinguishing features, and heavy focus on Amazon services failed to attract users in a market dominated by Apple and Android.

15.3 Cross-Platform Compatibility: A Divisive Issue

WebGL's success can be attributed, in part, to its broad cross-platform support. It is well-supported across all major browsers and operating systems, allowing developers to create applications that run consistently on a wide range of devices. WebGPU, however, is still in the early stages of adoption, and its cross-platform support is not as comprehensive. While efforts are being made to ensure WebGPU works on all major browsers and operating systems, discrepancies in performance and feature support across platforms remain a significant issue. This lack of consistency poses a challenge for developers who need their applications to run smoothly on multiple devices.

15.3.1 WebGL's Cross-Platform Dominance

WebGL has set the standard for cross-platform web graphics, with near-universal support across browsers and operating systems. Whether on Windows, macOS, Linux, or mobile devices, developers can rely on WebGL to deliver consistent results. This wide support has made WebGL the go-to choice for developers creating web-based 3D graphics applications. In contrast, WebGPU's cross-platform support is still a work in progress. While some browsers, like Chrome and Firefox, have implemented WebGPU support, others are lagging behind. Additionally, differences in GPU drivers across platforms can lead to inconsistent performance and behavior, further complicating WebGPU's cross-platform ambitions.

15.3.2 WebGPU's Fragmented Rollout

Despite the promise of WebGPU, its rollout has been fragmented and inconsistent. Some platforms and browsers have been quick to adopt WebGPU, while others are slower to implement it. This fragmented adoption creates uncertainty for developers, who may not be able to rely on WebGPU being available on all devices their users are running. Moreover, even on platforms where WebGPU is supported, there can be significant performance disparities due to differences in GPU drivers, operating systems, and hardware. These inconsistencies make it difficult for developers to create applications that perform consistently across different environments, further reducing WebGPU's appeal compared to the more stable and widely supported WebGL.

15.4 The Future of Web Graphics: Is WebGPU the Right Direction?

WebGPU represents a significant evolution in web graphics, offering developers more control and the potential for higher performance. However, the complexities associated with its use, combined with its inconsistent adoption across platforms, raise questions about whether it is the right direction for the future of web graphics. While WebGPU is undeniably more powerful than WebGL, it may not be the best solution for all use cases, particularly for developers who prioritize ease of use and broad compatibility.

The web development community must weigh the benefits of WebGPU's increased performance against the costs of its complexity and fragmented support.

15.4.1 The Case for WebGL's Continued Relevance

Despite WebGPU's advances, WebGL is far from obsolete. For many developers, WebGL remains a more practical choice due to its simplicity, stability, and widespread adoption. WebGL's ease of use allows developers to quickly create 3D graphics applications without needing to delve into the complexities of low-level GPU programming. Moreover, WebGL's continued support across all major browsers ensures that developers can reach a broad audience without worrying about platform-specific issues. For simpler applications and projects where high performance is not the primary concern, WebGL is likely to remain a popular choice for the foreseeable future.

15.5 Summary

WebGPU's future success depends on overcoming several challenges, including improving cross-platform support, simplifying the API for developers, and ensuring consistent performance across different environments. While WebGPU offers significant potential for high-performance web graphics, it is still a young technology that has not yet reached the level of maturity and adoption that WebGL enjoys. Developers will need to weigh the benefits of WebGPU's power and flexibility against the complexities and challenges it introduces. Ultimately, WebGPU has the potential to shape the future of web graphics, but its success will depend on how quickly the web development ecosystem can adapt to its demands.

16
Chapter

Behind the Curtain: Who Really Benefits from WebGPU?

Quote: "If you don't build your dream, someone else will hire you to help them build theirs." (**Tony Gaskins**)

16.1 Introduction

On the surface, WebGPU might seem like the natural evolution of web graphics—an advancement we've been waiting for. But dig a little deeper, and a different story starts to emerge. A story of vested interests, hidden agendas, and powerful companies eager to capitalize on the shift. While WebGPU is being marketed as the future of web development, there's a question we should all be asking: *who truly stands to gain from this so-called revolution?*

Let's look at the facts. WebGPU is designed to leverage the latest and greatest in GPU hardware, promising faster, more efficient graphics. But here's the catch—it demands new technology. It pushes for cutting-edge GPUs that the average user might not have today, forcing developers and consumers alike to upgrade. Older GPUs, which WebGL supported just fine, are now being left behind.

This shift isn't just an unfortunate consequence of progress—it's a gold mine for companies like NVIDIA, who manufacture these high-end GPUs. By pushing WebGPU as the standard, they've ensured that anyone serious about staying at the forefront of web development will have to invest in newer, pricier hardware. The more WebGPU is integrated into the web ecosystem, the more pressure there is on developers and users to upgrade. And who do these upgrades benefit the most? The very companies whose profits depend on selling the latest GPUs.

Meanwhile, WebGL—despite its age—continues to support a broader range of hardware, including older generations of GPUs. Had WebGL remained the dominant web graphics API, companies like NVIDIA would face a different reality. Older hardware would still need support, meaning fewer users and developers would feel the urgent need to buy into the newest tech. WebGL's long tail of backward compatibility didn't serve their bottom line, but it served the everyday user well. WebGPU, on the other hand, conveniently narrows that compatibility window, cutting off older devices and pushing everyone toward the next wave of hardware.

Of course, none of this is mentioned in the glossy marketing materials for WebGPU. Instead, we hear about "next-gen graphics," "performance gains," and "future-proofing." These are all buzzwords that sound appealing but mask the true cost of this transition.

Who's actually driving the WebGPU train? It's not just developers eager for new features. Look at the major players behind the push—hardware manufacturers, GPU vendors, and even some browser companies, all of whom stand to make a fortune as users and developers are nudged—or shoved—toward new hardware.

It's easy to see WebGPU as the inevitable next step in web graphics, but when you peel back the layers, it becomes clear that there's more going on. The sudden rush to adopt this new API isn't just about innovation—it's about money. A lot of money. And the people who stand to make the most are the ones whose hardware you'll need to keep up.

Could WebGPU have been built differently? Absolutely. It could have been designed with broader hardware support, with a focus on keeping older technologies in the fold, much like WebGL did. But that's not the direction we've gone in. Instead, we have an API that caters to the high-end, leaving many older devices behind and creating a cycle of forced upgrades.

16.2 The Illusion of Open Standards: Who Really Has the Say?

WebGPU is presented as an open standard, championed by the W3C and developed in collaboration with major browser vendors and hardware manufacturers. On the surface, this paints a picture of community-driven progress—an API designed for the benefit of all. However, behind the scenes, the reality is more complicated. While WebGPU is technically an open standard, its development is heavily influenced by the financial interests of large corporations that control the direction of both hardware and software. These players—companies like Google, Apple, Microsoft, and major GPU vendors such as NVIDIA and AMD—hold significant sway in the decision-making process. Their financial clout and market power ensure that WebGPU evolves in a way that aligns with their business goals, rather than purely benefiting developers or end-users.

This influence is particularly evident when looking at how WebGPU prioritizes certain features or hardware capabilities that serve the interests of these corporations. For instance, WebGPU's close ties to modern GPU architectures ensure that it works best with the latest hardware, which benefits companies selling high-end devices. In this sense, while WebGPU may be open on paper, the reality is that its development is steered by entities with much to gain from its success—entities whose motivations are more profit-driven than altruistic.

16.3 Targeting the Rich: A Tool for High-End Development

While WebGPU aims to revolutionize web-based graphics by offering low-level access to GPU resources, the truth is that it is not a democratizing technology for all developers. Instead, it appears to target a wealthier demographic of developers and users—those working on cutting-edge, resource-intensive projects like AAA games, real-time simulations, and virtual reality. These types of applications require significant hardware power, and WebGPU is designed to unlock that power, but only if the hardware is there to support it.

The average web developer, working on simpler 2D graphics or web applications, might find little reason to adopt WebGPU, as its complexity and steep hardware requirements make it overkill for many tasks. In this way, WebGPU is not an API for everyone; it is largely aimed at developers who are already working with, or can afford, high-end hardware and have the expertise to leverage its capabilities. For those targeting the high-performance computing or gaming markets, WebGPU may be a boon. But for the vast majority of developers, especially those in less resource-intensive fields, WebGPU's complexity and hardware demands create more barriers than opportunities.

16.4 The High Cost of Free: Hardware Isn't Free, and Neither Is WebGPU

Though WebGPU is free to use, the hardware required to fully take advantage of its capabilities is anything but. The push towards WebGPU is part of a broader trend in the tech industry where new APIs and software updates push consumers to purchase ever-more powerful and expensive hardware. WebGPU demands modern GPU architectures, which in turn means that developers and end-users need to invest in expensive graphics cards, processors, and high-performance systems to make full use of the technology.

This is particularly concerning because it undermines one of the foundational promises of web technologies: accessibility. Historically, the web has been accessible on a wide range of devices, from low-powered laptops to high-end workstations. WebGPU, however, threatens to change this dynamic by prioritizing performance over accessibility, effectively making high-end hardware a prerequisite for modern web development. This creates a divide between those who can afford the latest devices and those who cannot, further entrenching inequality in the tech space.

> **Food for Thought** - Innovative Technologies That Fell Short: **Clippy** (1997) - The Infamous Microsoft Office Assistant - Microsoft's animated paperclip assistant, Clippy, was designed to help users with Office tasks. However, it quickly became notorious for being intrusive and unhelpful, leading to widespread dislike and eventual retirement.

16.5 Pushing the Upgrade Cycle: Encouraging New Hardware Purchases

One of the most significant, albeit subtle, effects of WebGPU's introduction is its role in driving hardware upgrades. By designing the API to favor the capabilities of modern GPUs, WebGPU incentivizes both developers and consumers to upgrade their hardware. Developers working on performance-intensive applications like games or VR experiences will find that older systems simply cannot keep up with the demands of WebGPU, forcing them to invest in newer, more powerful machines. In turn, as developers create more complex and visually impressive content using WebGPU, end-users will also need to upgrade their systems to experience these applications as intended.

This constant cycle of upgrading benefits hardware manufacturers significantly. Every few years, new software standards emerge that push hardware to its limits, effectively shortening the lifecycle of existing devices. WebGPU plays a key role in this cycle by establishing itself as the future of web graphics, but at a cost—forcing consumers and developers to continually purchase new hardware to stay current. While WebGPU promises to unlock new creative possibilities, it does so at the expense of making older hardware obsolete more quickly than ever before.

16.6 Who Really Benefits: The Corporations Behind WebGPU

In the end, the true beneficiaries of WebGPU are not the developers or users, but the corporations that profit from hardware sales and control the future of web technologies. Companies like NVIDIA, AMD, Intel, and major tech giants like Google and Apple stand to gain the most from WebGPU's adoption. By creating a new standard that favors the latest hardware, these companies ensure that they remain at the forefront of the technology industry, reaping the financial rewards of increased hardware sales and subscription-based cloud services that can leverage WebGPU's capabilities.

The narrative that WebGPU is a revolutionary open standard that will democratize web-based GPU access is, to some extent, misleading. The reality is that WebGPU, like many technological advancements, serves the interests of large corporations far more than it serves the broader developer community. The push for WebGPU adoption ultimately benefits those who have the most to gain from selling the hardware and services necessary to support its use, leaving the average developer and consumer to bear the financial burden of keeping up with its demands.

16.7 Summary

Looking ahead, WebGPU's future may well be defined by the divide it creates between high-end and average users. Unless efforts are made to ensure that WebGPU remains accessible on a wide range of hardware, it risks becoming a tool reserved for an elite group of developers working with cutting-edge technology. As the API continues to evolve, it will be crucial to strike a balance between pushing the boundaries of GPU programming and maintaining accessibility for all developers. If WebGPU fails to achieve this balance, it may end up serving the interests of corporations more than the broader web development community.

17
Chapter

Surviving the Disaster: Finding Solutions in the Chaos

Quote: "The only real mistake is the one from which we learn nothing." (**Henry Ford**)

17.1 Introduction

The promise of WebGPU was to provide a modern, efficient, and powerful interface for accessing GPUs across multiple platforms. However, the reality has fallen short in several critical areas. Performance bottlenecks, inconsistent cross-platform support, and debugging nightmares are just a few of the hurdles developers encounter. These problems stem from the inherent complexity of the API and its close relationship with GPU hardware, which introduces challenges that simpler APIs like WebGL do not have. A clear assessment of these shortcomings helps developers set realistic expectations and adjust their approach accordingly.

The areas where WebGPU falters most severely—performance degradation, lack of robust debugging tools, and platform-specific inconsistencies—are also the areas that directly impact developers' productivity. Developers accustomed to WebGL's relative ease of use often find themselves frustrated with the steep learning curve and additional complexity. Additionally, the limited tooling and documentation make resolving these issues even more difficult. Identifying which areas cause the most friction for specific projects allows teams to focus their efforts on targeted solutions rather than becoming bogged down by the entirety of WebGPU's challenges.

17.2 Strategies for Overcoming WebGPU's Shortcomings

Despite the many obstacles presented by WebGPU, there are viable strategies to mitigate its impact on development processes. By taking advantage of existing tools, adopting best practices from similar APIs, and working within WebGPU's current limitations, developers can find ways to make the best of a difficult situation. While WebGPU may not be perfect, it still offers powerful capabilities for developers willing to adapt.

17.2.1 Leveraging Community Resources: Working Together to Solve Problems

One of the most valuable resources in navigating WebGPU's complexities is the developer community itself. WebGPU's open-source nature means that many developers are actively sharing their experiences, solutions, and workarounds for common problems. By participating in forums, contributing to open-source projects, and sharing knowledge through blogs and conferences, developers can help each other overcome the steep learning curve. Collaboration across the community has already led to the creation of debugging tools, documentation supplements, and even performance optimization strategies that aren't covered in official resources.

17.2.2 Adopting Best Practices: Learning from Other APIs

Though WebGPU introduces new paradigms for GPU programming, developers can draw on best practices from existing APIs like Vulkan, Metal, and DirectX. These APIs share similar concepts with WebGPU in terms of resource management, memory allocation, and command buffering. Developers familiar with these APIs can apply their knowledge to improve efficiency when working with WebGPU. Furthermore, lessons learned from these lower-level APIs regarding synchronization, threading, and performance optimization can be adapted for use in WebGPU applications. This cross-pollination of practices allows developers to apply tried-and-tested solutions to WebGPU's emerging issues.

17.2.3 Embracing Incremental Adoption: When to Use WebGPU

Not every project needs to dive headfirst into WebGPU. For many applications, sticking with WebGL or a hybrid approach—leveraging WebGPU only where its capabilities are genuinely necessary—can be a more pragmatic path. WebGPU excels in scenarios requiring high-performance compute tasks, fine-grained GPU control, and more complex rendering techniques, such as real-time simulations and VR applications. However, for simpler 3D rendering or web-based games, the additional complexity of WebGPU may not justify the transition. Understanding when to embrace WebGPU and when to stick with WebGL helps ensure developers don't adopt WebGPU prematurely or unnecessarily.

17.3 Tools and Techniques for Troubleshooting

One of the most daunting aspects of working with WebGPU is the lack of comprehensive tools for debugging and performance analysis. However, even within these limitations, there are ways to improve the debugging process and troubleshoot more effectively. With the right techniques and external tools, developers can make sense of WebGPU's cryptic errors and work through performance bottlenecks in a structured manner.

> **Food for Thought** - Innovative Technologies That Fell Short: **Apple Pippin** (1996) - Apple's Forgotten Gaming Console - Apple's Pippin was an attempt to merge gaming and computing into a multimedia platform. However, it was overpriced, underpowered compared to its gaming competitors, and lacked strong software support, resulting in very low sales.

17.3.1 Developing Custom Debugging Tools: Taking Control of the Process

Given the immaturity of WebGPU's debugging ecosystem, many developers are resorting to building their own tools or extending existing ones. Tools like Chrome's built-in DevTools or external profiling software designed for WebGL can be adapted for WebGPU use. Additionally, custom debugging frameworks that log GPU state, memory usage, and command buffer execution can help developers trace issues more effectively. While building these tools requires extra effort, they can dramatically reduce the time spent hunting for bugs in complex GPU applications.

17.3.2 Profiling and Performance Monitoring: Identifying Bottlenecks

Performance bottlenecks in WebGPU can be difficult to diagnose without proper profiling tools. However, some techniques, such as instrumenting code with timers or using browser-based performance analyzers, can provide insight into where the application is slowing down. Monitoring GPU load, CPU-GPU synchronization times, and memory usage can help pinpoint inefficiencies. While comprehensive tools like those available for native APIs are still missing for WebGPU, creative use of existing tools can make performance monitoring feasible, even in the early stages of WebGPU's lifecycle.

17.4 Long-Term Solutions: Pushing WebGPU Forward

WebGPU's future success depends largely on overcoming the current limitations that make it difficult to use and troubleshoot. In the long term, both the community and industry players need to invest in improving WebGPU's usability, tooling, and cross-platform support to ensure that it reaches its full potential. The good news is that WebGPU, like any emerging technology, has room to evolve, and these issues are not insurmountable. By continuing to refine the API, building out a better ecosystem of tools, and pushing for broader platform support, WebGPU could become a stable and powerful platform for web-based GPU programming.

17.4.1 The Role of Standardization: Improving Cross-Platform Consistency

One of the most critical aspects of WebGPU's success will be ensuring a more consistent experience across platforms. Standardization efforts are already underway, but these efforts need to be accelerated and expanded to ensure that WebGPU performs consistently across different browsers, operating systems, and hardware. GPU vendors must also improve their support for WebGPU by providing reliable drivers and timely updates. Without these improvements, developers will continue to face fragmentation and inconsistency in their WebGPU applications.

17.4.2 Tooling Evolution: The Path to Better Debugging and Performance Analysis

To make WebGPU more accessible, better debugging and profiling tools are essential. The current lack of comprehensive debugging tools is a significant barrier to adoption, and it is crucial that the browser vendors and developer community prioritize the creation of these tools. Over time, we can expect to see more sophisticated debugging frameworks and performance analyzers emerge, making it easier for developers to troubleshoot and optimize their WebGPU applications. These tools will be essential in pushing WebGPU forward and making it a viable choice for more developers.

17.5 Summary

Although WebGPU's challenges are significant, they are not insurmountable. By embracing community collaboration, adopting best practices from other APIs, and pushing for better tooling and standardization, developers can navigate the current chaos and find practical solutions. While the path forward is not without obstacles, WebGPU holds great promise, and with continued investment from both the community and industry, it can eventually reach its potential as the future of web-based graphics programming.

Appendix